Royal JUMBLE®

Majestic puzzles that reign supreme!

Henri Arnold,
Jeff Knurek,
and
Mike Argirion

TRIUMPH
BOOKS

This book is available in quantity at special discounts
for your group or organization.

For further information, contact:

Triumph Books LLC
814 North Franklin Street
Chicago, Illinois 60610
(800) 888-4741

Printed in U.S.A.

ISBN: 978-1-60078-738-6

Design by Sue Knopf

Contents

Royal JUMBLE®

Classic
Puzzles

JUMBLE®

Unscramble these four Jumbles, one letter to each square, to form four ordinary words.

TABLO

HAFES

UMLUTT

GURFAL

Hurry! We've only got 4 hours left to put it together

'18

WHEN THE SPEED TEAM PREPARED FOR THE BIG DRAG RACE, THEY WENT----

Now arrange the circled letters to form the surprise answer, as suggested by the above cartoon.

Print answer here

" "

JUMBLE®

Unscramble these four Jumbles, one letter to each square, to form four ordinary words.

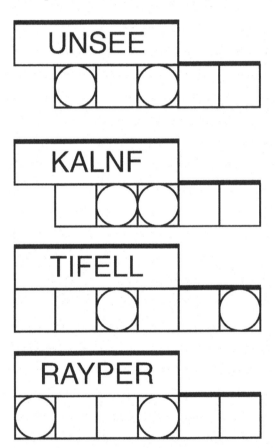

UNSEE

KALNF

TIFELL

RAYPER

WHAT HE SAW WHEN HE VISITED THE PRINT SHOP.

Now arrange the circled letters to form the surprise answer, as suggested by the above cartoon.

Print answer here

3

JUMBLE®

Unscramble these four Jumbles, one letter to each square, to form four ordinary words.

ZALBE

REDEL

RUGBBY

VENNIT

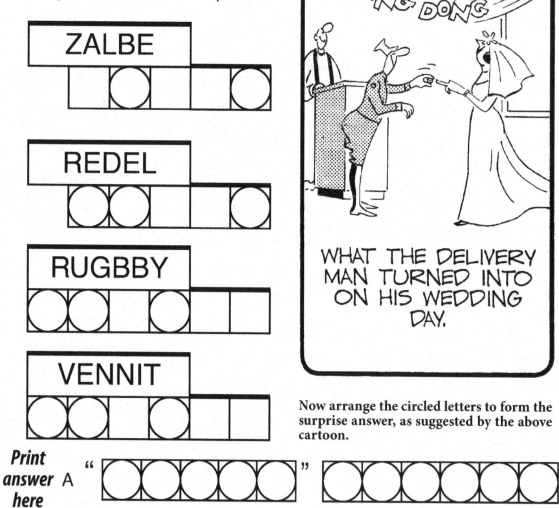

DING DONG

WHAT THE DELIVERY MAN TURNED INTO ON HIS WEDDING DAY.

Now arrange the circled letters to form the surprise answer, as suggested by the above cartoon.

Print answer A here "◯◯◯◯◯" ◯◯◯◯◯◯◯

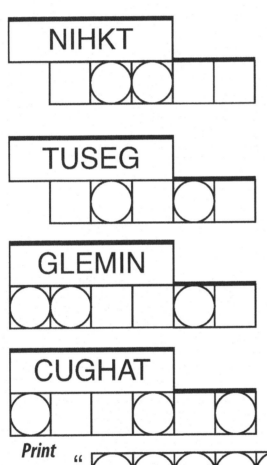

JUMBLE®

Unscramble these four Jumbles, one letter to each square, to form four ordinary words.

NIHKT

TUSEG

GLEMIN

CUGHAT

Good thing my player runs on batteries

This is romantic

ENJOYED BY THE COUPLE WHEN THE POWER FAILED.

Now arrange the circled letters to form the surprise answer, as suggested by the above cartoon.

Print answer here   " ⭕⭕⭕⭕⭕ "   ⭕⭕⭕⭕⭕

JUMBLE®

Unscramble these four Jumbles, one letter to each square, to form four ordinary words.

WEPOR

UNDEC

HUBLES

YURETS

— Touchdown! North wins

WHAT THE RUNNING BACK DID AS TIME WAS RUNNING OUT.

Now arrange the circled letters to form the surprise answer, as suggested by the above cartoon.

Print answer here " ⬡⬡⬡⬡⬡⬡ " TO ⬡⬡⬡⬡⬡

JUMBLE®

Unscramble these four Jumbles, one letter to each square, to form four ordinary words.

THILG

RAMOA

INTADE

TAKEGS

You didn't learn your tables. Extra — homework tonight

WHAT THE PUPILS EXPERIENCED WHEN THEY FAILED THE MULTIPLICATION TEST.

Now arrange the circled letters to form the surprise answer, as suggested by the above cartoon.

Print answer here

JUMBLE®

Unscramble these four Jumbles, one letter to each square, to form four ordinary words.

STUQE

GUNED

TADISS

STIJUR

No treats for a week

WHEN THE TWINS ATE MOM'S PARTY CUPCAKES, THEY GOT THEIR----

Now arrange the circled letters to form the surprise answer, as suggested by the above cartoon.

Print answer here

"   "

JUMBLE®

Unscramble these four Jumbles, one letter to each square, to form four ordinary words.

TUDOO

LUMPE

LOOSCH

FENTAS

YOU MIGHT SAY THE "HOT" MOVIE DID THIS TO THE MATRONS.

Now arrange the circled letters to form the surprise answer, as suggested by the above cartoon.

Print answer here

JUMBLE®

Unscramble these four Jumbles, one letter to each square, to form four ordinary words.

EUQER

OCCIL

ROPPEH

SHRUPE

He sits there every day

WHERE THE FISHER-MAN COULD ALWAYS BE FOUND.

Now arrange the circled letters to form the surprise answer, as suggested by the above cartoon.

Print answer here ON HIS ◯◯◯◯◯ ◯◯◯◯◯

JUMBLE®

Unscramble these four Jumbles, one letter to each square, to form four ordinary words.

TEVEN

VORSA

CUBLEK

TRUBLE

I want to make sure everything is even

A GOOD CARPEN-TER WILL DO THIS.

Now arrange the circled letters to form the surprise answer, as suggested by the above cartoon.

Print answer here   HIS "◯◯◯◯◯" ◯◯◯◯

JUMBLE®

Unscramble these four Jumbles, one letter to each square, to form four ordinary words.

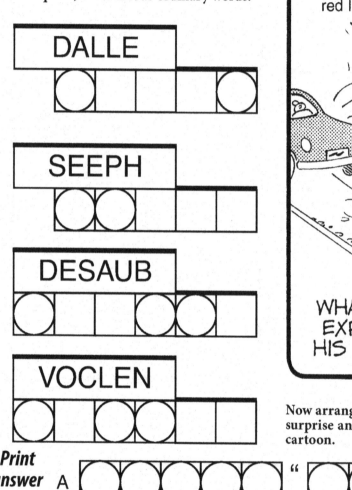

DALLE

SEEPH

DESAUB

VOCLEN

He ran a red light

WHAT THE BARBER EXPERIENCED ON HIS WAY TO WORK.

Now arrange the circled letters to form the surprise answer, as suggested by the above cartoon.

Print answer here

A  "  "

JUMBLE®

Unscramble these four Jumbles, one letter to each square, to form four ordinary words.

TROIB

YESTT

SORIAL

KRANET

Like this, Sarge?

WHAT THE RECRUIT DID WHEN BAYONET TRAINING BEGAN.

Now arrange the circled letters to form the surprise answer, as suggested by the above cartoon.

Print answer here

⬡⬡⬡⬡ A " ⬡⬡⬡⬡⬡ " ⬡⬡ IT

JUMBLE®

Unscramble these four Jumbles, one letter to
each square, to form four ordinary words.

NAVER

HASQU

BELBUB

NULRUY

I say there. My,
but you're loverly

WHAT A LONDONER
USES FOR A "LINE."

Now arrange the circled letters to form the
surprise answer, as suggested by the above
cartoon.

Print answer here   A "◯◯◯◯◯"

14

JUMBLE®

Unscramble these four Jumbles, one letter to each square, to form four ordinary words.

LEVED

NICCY

REATEA

VAQUER

Now turn the lens until the image is sharp

WHEN THE NOVICE WAS TAUGHT HOW TO FOCUS, THE INSTRUCTIONS WERE----

Now arrange the circled letters to form the surprise answer, as suggested by the above cartoon.

Print answer here ⬡⬡⬡⬡⬡ " ⬡⬡⬡⬡⬡ "

JUMBLE®

Unscramble these four Jumbles, one letter to each square, to form four ordinary words.

NILTE

NECEP

NAVIED

SIFOSY

Are we done yet?

Stand still!

WHAT THE BOY EXPERIENCED WHEN HE WAS FITTED FOR A SUIT.

Now arrange the circled letters to form the surprise answer, as suggested by the above cartoon.

Print answer here

 AND

JUMBLE®

Unscramble these four Jumbles, one letter to each square, to form four ordinary words.

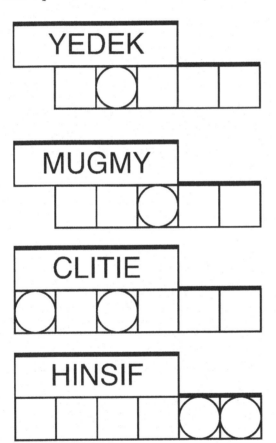

YEDEK

MUGMY

CLITIE

HINSIF

How 'bout dinner... perhaps a movie

E

WHAT SHE DECIDED WHEN THE EYE DOCTOR ASKED HER OUT.

Now arrange the circled letters to form the surprise answer, as suggested by the above cartoon.

Print answer here   TO "  "

JUMBLE®

Unscramble these four Jumbles, one letter to
each square, to form four ordinary words.

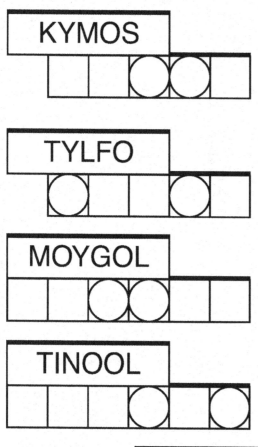

KYMOS

TYLFO

MOYGOL

TINOOL

NUDIST CAMP

WHEN HE WAS TOLD
ABOUT THE HOLE
IN THE WALL, THE
COP SAID HE'D----

Now arrange the circled letters to form the
surprise answer, as suggested by the above
cartoon.

Print answer
here "  "  IT

JUMBLE®

Unscramble these four Jumbles, one letter to
each square, to form four ordinary words.

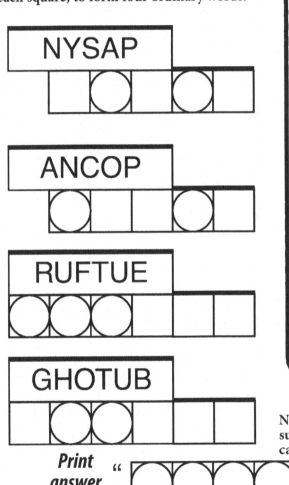

NYSAP

ANCOP

RUFTUE

GHOTUB

This digital
camera does
all the work

WHAT THE PHO-
TOGRAPHER USED
TO TAKE PICTURES
OF THE NEW CAR.

Now arrange the circled letters to form the
surprise answer, as suggested by the above
cartoon.

*Print
answer
here*

" ◯◯◯◯ " ◯◯◯◯◯

JUMBLE®

Unscramble these four Jumbles, one letter to
each square, to form four ordinary words.

RIDUL

YAFOR

TARROM

REBAWE

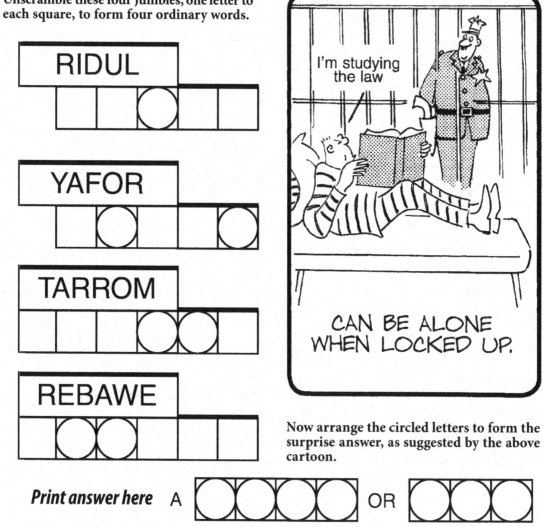

I'm studying
the law

CAN BE ALONE
WHEN LOCKED UP.

Now arrange the circled letters to form the
surprise answer, as suggested by the above
cartoon.

Print answer here A ⬡⬡⬡⬡ OR ⬡⬡⬡

JUMBLE®

Unscramble these four Jumbles, one letter to
each square, to form four ordinary words.

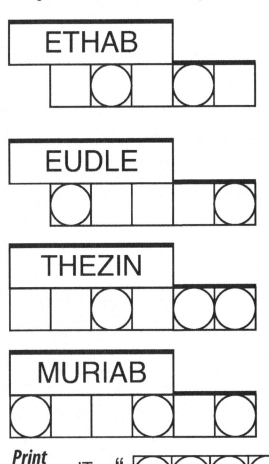

ETHAB

EUDLE

THEZIN

MURIAB

Come take a look

No, thanks. I'll stick to the sky

WHY THE FIGHTER
PILOT REFUSED
TO TOUR THE
SUBMARINE.

Now arrange the circled letters to form the
surprise answer, as suggested by the above
cartoon.

Print
answer
here
IT
WAS
" ⬡⬡⬡⬡⬡⬡⬡ " ⬡⬡⬡

21

JUMBLE®

Unscramble these four Jumbles, one letter to each square, to form four ordinary words.

RONED

ENMOY

BRAMKE

TECJOB

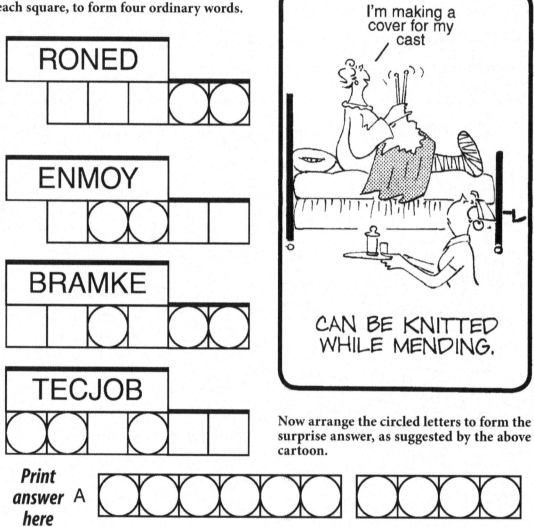

I'm making a cover for my cast

CAN BE KNITTED WHILE MENDING.

Now arrange the circled letters to form the surprise answer, as suggested by the above cartoon.

Print answer here A ⬡⬡⬡⬡⬡⬡ ⬡⬡⬡⬡

JUMBLE®

Unscramble these four Jumbles, one letter to each square, to form four ordinary words.

LORBI

SYSMO

SWILEY

GANTEM

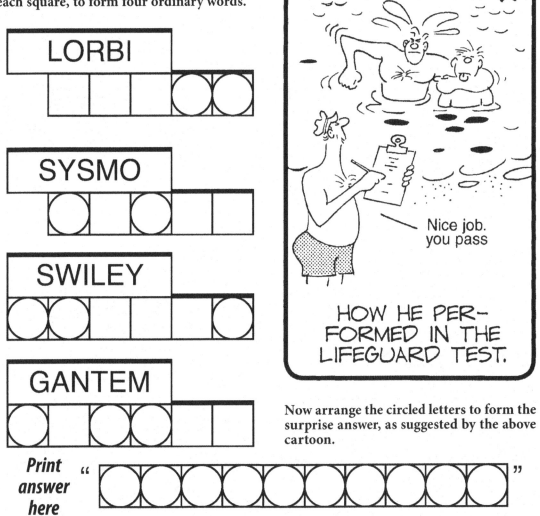

Nice job. you pass

HOW HE PER-
FORMED IN THE
LIFEGUARD TEST.

Now arrange the circled letters to form the surprise answer, as suggested by the above cartoon.

Print answer here " ⬡⬡⬡⬡⬡⬡⬡⬡⬡⬡⬡ "

JUMBLE®

Unscramble these four Jumbles, one letter to
each square, to form four ordinary words.

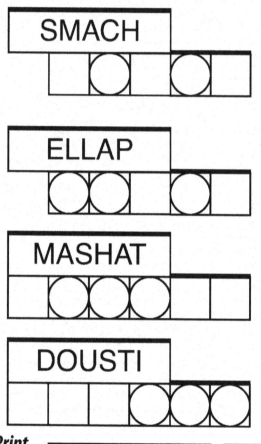

SMACH

ELLAP

MASHAT

DOUSTI

Time to go home, Edgar

WHEN THE TIPSY
PARTYGOER WORE
A LAMPSHADE, HIS
WIFE SAID HE'D----

Now arrange the circled letters to form the
surprise answer, as suggested by the above
cartoon.

**Print
answer
here**

JUMBLE

Unscramble these four Jumbles, one letter to each square, to form four ordinary words.

UGGOE

NARFC

TANFUL

GLINKY

Climbing to 5,000 feet

WHEN THE STRIPPER LEARNED TO FLY, SHE WAS GOOD AT THIS.

Now arrange the circled letters to form the surprise answer, as suggested by the above cartoon.

Print answer here

JUMBLE®

Unscramble these four Jumbles, one letter to each square, to form four ordinary words.

DEKIN

VELGO

SHEARE

THODEB

Maybe you can just roll it up

WHAT THE KNITTERS DID WHEN SHE MADE THE SLEEVES UNEVEN.

Now arrange the circled letters to form the surprise answer, as suggested by the above cartoon.

Print answer here " ⬡⬡⬡⬡⬡⬡⬡ " ⬡⬡⬡

Royal JUMBLE

Daily Puzzles

JUMBLE®

Unscramble these four Jumbles, one letter to
each square, to form four ordinary words.

CORUS

GYLUL

DOLSUN

YARNLE

He's had four
Broadway hits

He stays
in shape

THE PRODUCER
ENTERED THE
MARATHON RACE
BECAUSE HE WAS
GOOD AT----

Now arrange the circled letters to form the
surprise answer, as suggested by the above
cartoon.

*Print answer
here*   ◯◯◯◯ " ◯◯◯◯ "

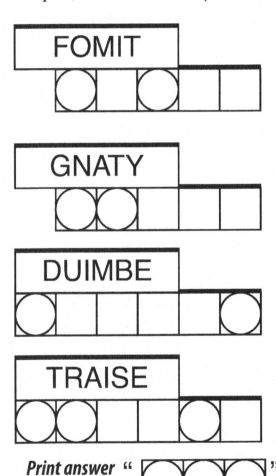

JUMBLE®

Unscramble these four Jumbles, one letter to each square, to form four ordinary words.

FOMIT

GNATY

DUIMBE

TRAISE

That doesn't look like me!

Now listen here, you old...

WHEN SHE REFUSED TO PAY FOR HER PORTRAIT, HE TURNED INTO A----

Now arrange the circled letters to form the surprise answer, as suggested by the above cartoon.

Print answer " ⬡⬡⬡ " ⬡⬡⬡⬡⬡⬡
here

JUMBLE®

Unscramble these four Jumbles, one letter to each square, to form four ordinary words.

AUFAN

VUCER

REYMOB

TINTEN

This isn't a real $100 bill

That's as good as gold!

WHEN THE SHOPPER WAS ACCUSED OF PASSING PHONY MONEY, HE HAD A——

Now arrange the circled letters to form the surprise answer, as suggested by the above cartoon.

Print answer here

JUMBLE®

Unscramble these four Jumbles, one letter to each square, to form four ordinary words.

NOFET

OUSLE

DRIZAL

ROWMAR

So much for that old pillow

WHEN THE GOOSE FEATHERS FLEW UP AND AWAY, THEY WERE---

Now arrange the circled letters to form the surprise answer, as suggested by the above cartoon.

Print answer here

◯◯◯◯◯ " ◯◯◯◯ "

31

JUMBLE®

Unscramble these four Jumbles, one letter to
each square, to form four ordinary words.

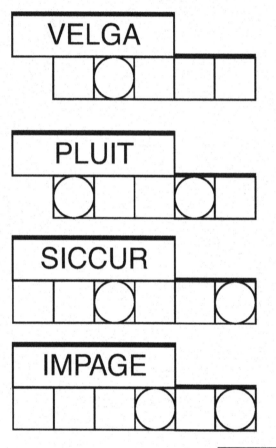

VELGA

PLUIT

SICCUR

IMPAGE

"PIRATES" CAN
GIVE YOU THIS

Now arrange the circled letters to form the
surprise answer, as suggested by the above
cartoon.

Print answer here

JUMBLE®

Unscramble these four Jumbles, one letter to each square, to form four ordinary words.

LUKKS

RUPOC

HOMIDS

GANTOU

Isn't she gorgeous?

WHAT THE CAT SHOW WINNER TURNED INTO ---

Now arrange the circled letters to form the surprise answer, as suggested by the above cartoon.

Print answer here   A ⬡⬡⬡⬡⬡⬡⬡ " ⬡⬡⬡⬡ "

JUMBLE®

Unscramble these four Jumbles, one letter to
each square, to form four ordinary words.

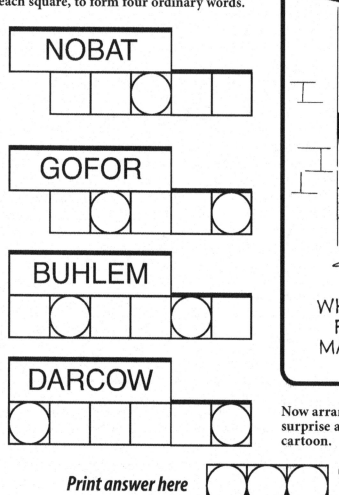

NOBAT

GOFOR

BUHLEM

DARCOW

Are you O.K.?

WHEN THE ICICLE
FELL ON THE
MAILMAN'S HEAD,
HE WAS ---

Now arrange the circled letters to form the
surprise answer, as suggested by the above
cartoon.

Print answer here  " "

34

JUMBLE®

Unscramble these four Jumbles, one letter to each square, to form four ordinary words.

VARFO

SACEE

JORNAG

VILDER

An ace!
He wins

THE WAITER WON
THE TENNIS MATCH
BECAUSE HE
WAS A ‒‒‒

Now arrange the circled letters to form the surprise answer, as suggested by the above cartoon.

Print answer here [◯◯◯◯] " [◯◯◯◯◯◯] "

JUMBLE®

Unscramble these four Jumbles, one letter to each square, to form four ordinary words.

RILCY

TEYIP

ORFALL

INSEPP

I'm playing a sneaky character

THE ACTOR USED GREASEPAINT BECAUSE HE HAD A ----

Now arrange the circled letters to form the surprise answer, as suggested by the above cartoon.

Print answer here

"  "

JUMBLE®

Unscramble these four Jumbles, one letter to each square, to form four ordinary words.

SYHIF

BIGEE

ZYNEEM

CLIFEA

LIBRARY

You can talk all you want

ADVICE THAT ISN'T SOUND.

Now arrange the circled letters to form the surprise answer, as suggested by the above cartoon.

Print answer here

37

JUMBLE®

Unscramble these four Jumbles, one letter to each square, to form four ordinary words.

PONCA

SURBT

THRENE

PERRIM

IT TAKES MORE THAN ONE TO RUN THIS KIND OF BUSINESS.

Now arrange the circled letters to form the surprise answer, as suggested by the above cartoon.

Print answer here A ☐☐☐☐☐☐☐☐☐☐☐☐

JUMBLE®

Unscramble these four Jumbles, one letter to each square, to form four ordinary words.

SULEO

YARIN

POOPSE

REGOFT

Keep your head down

ON A GOLF COURSE, MANY RICH GUYS CAN BE ----

Now arrange the circled letters to form the surprise answer, as suggested by the above cartoon.

Print answer here " ⬡⬡⬡⬡ " ⬡⬡⬡⬡⬡⬡⬡

JUMBLE®

Unscramble these four Jumbles, one letter to each square, to form four ordinary words.

TYFFI

TIARE

MOHGEA

NOMOIK

How does this look?
Maybe that one

WHAT HIS WIFE DID
WHEN SHE PICKED
OUT A WATCH.

Now arrange the circled letters to form the surprise answer, as suggested by the above cartoon.

Print answer here ◯◯◯◯ ◯◯◯ " ◯◯◯◯ "

JUMBLE®

Unscramble these four Jumbles, one letter to
each square, to form four ordinary words.

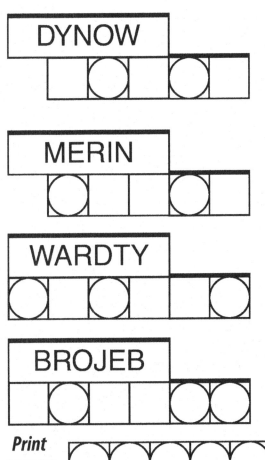

DYNOW

MERIN

WARDTY

BROJEB

WHAT THE STUDENT
WHO WANTED TO BE
AN AUTHOR DID.

Now arrange the circled letters to form the
surprise answer, as suggested by the above
cartoon.

Print
answer
here

FOR

JUMBLE®

Unscramble these four Jumbles, one letter to each square, to form four ordinary words.

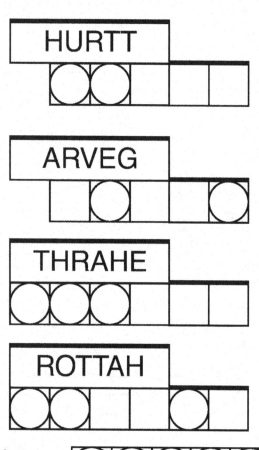

HURTT

ARVEG

THRAHE

ROTTAH

Watch your diet and get more exercise

You always say that

HOW HE DESCRIBED THE TALK WITH HIS CARDIOLOGIST.

Now arrange the circled letters to form the surprise answer, as suggested by the above cartoon.

Print answer here

 TO

JUMBLE®

Unscramble these four Jumbles, one letter to each square, to form four ordinary words.

SEGIN

CENAP

GIXNIF

TRUSEY

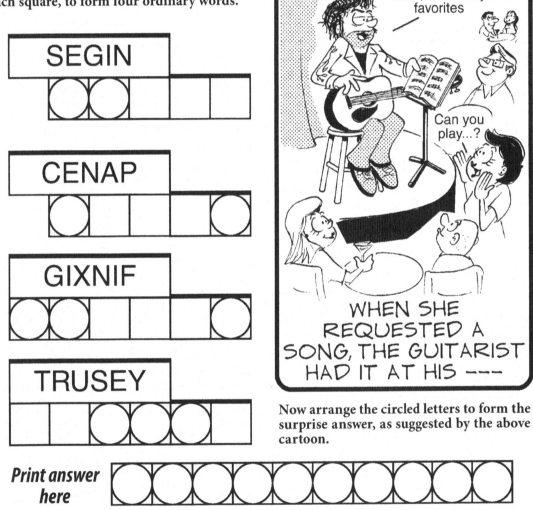

Sure, one of my favorites

Can you play...?

WHEN SHE REQUESTED A SONG, THE GUITARIST HAD IT AT HIS ---

Now arrange the circled letters to form the surprise answer, as suggested by the above cartoon.

Print answer here

JUMBLE

Unscramble these four Jumbles, one letter to each square, to form four ordinary words.

HAFIT

TASUE

DYSTUR

REVOUD

When they grow, I'll tie a hammock to them

WHAT THE MOBSTER FACED WHEN HE PLANTED THE TREES.

Now arrange the circled letters to form the surprise answer, as suggested by the above cartoon.

Print answer here A "  "

JUMBLE®

Unscramble these four Jumbles, one letter to each square, to form four ordinary words.

HYLYS

TAWLZ

SATTLE

DIVERF

I don't see my name

OBITUARIES

FOR MOST PEOPLE, OBITUARIES ARE THIS.

Now arrange the circled letters to form the surprise answer, as suggested by the above cartoon.

Print answer here   " "

JUMBLE®

Unscramble these four Jumbles, one letter to
each square, to form four ordinary words.

TORNS

SECAE

ROESIE

FLABEL

They always
have blouses
on sale

50%
OFF

YOU CAN FIND THIS
MARKED DOWN IN A
DEPARTMENT STORE.

Now arrange the circled letters to form the
surprise answer, as suggested by the above
cartoon.

**Print answer
here** AN ☐☐☐☐☐☐☐☐☐

JUMBLE®

Unscramble these four Jumbles, one letter to each square, to form four ordinary words.

BIANC

APITO

RELILK

LATOPS

What's the meaning of this?

WHAT THE STUDENTS BROUGHT TO SCHOOL FOR THEIR MEAN TEACHER

Now arrange the circled letters to form the surprise answer, as suggested by the above cartoon.

Print answer here " ☐☐☐☐ "   ☐☐☐☐☐☐☐

JUMBLE®

Unscramble these four Jumbles, one letter to each square, to form four ordinary words.

TILOP

FRATE

WILDEM

THINEW

Hello! May I buy you a drink?

THE GOLDDIGGER SNUBBED THE HAND- SOME PARTYGOER BECAUSE HE WASN'T ----

Now arrange the circled letters to form the surprise answer, as suggested by the above cartoon.

Print answer here

◯◯◯◯◯ HER " ◯◯◯◯ "

JUMBLE®

Unscramble these four Jumbles, one letter to each square, to form four ordinary words.

TIVER

STYRT

AGOVEY

FUELEY

Up and at 'em

WHAT A RINGING ALARM CLOCK CAN DO.

Now arrange the circled letters to form the surprise answer, as suggested by the above cartoon.

Print answer here

  A "  "

JUMBLE

Unscramble these four Jumbles, one letter to
each square, to form four ordinary words.

RAFIE
◯ ◯

LAKBY
◯ ◯ ◯

REBLUT
◯ ◯ ◯ ◯

SLARIO
◯ ◯

I've got another
dollar here somewhere

AFTER PAYING FOR
THE TIRE CHANGE,
HE WAS ----

Now arrange the circled letters to form the
surprise answer, as suggested by the above
cartoon.

Print answer
here
" ◯ ◯ ◯ ◯ ◯ " ◯ ◯ ◯ ◯ ◯ ◯

JUMBLE®

Unscramble these four Jumbles, one letter to
each square, to form four ordinary words.

EUTCH

VAYEH

DINBAT

QUIROL

We'll have to
hire another crew

WHAT THE TREE
TRIMMERS DID WHEN
THEY GOT THE
BIG JOB.

Now arrange the circled letters to form the
surprise answer, as suggested by the above
cartoon.

Print
answer
here   " ⬡⬡⬡⬡⬡⬡⬡⬡ "   ⬡⬡⬡

JUMBLE®

Unscramble these four Jumbles, one letter to each square, to form four ordinary words.

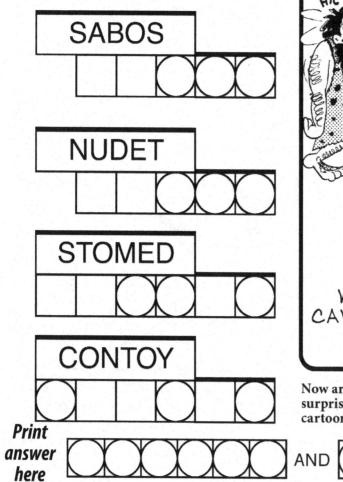

SABOS

NUDET

STOMED

CONTOY

WHEN THE TIPSY CAVEMAN GOT HOME, HE WAS ----

Now arrange the circled letters to form the surprise answer, as suggested by the above cartoon.

Print answer here

AND

JUMBLE®

Unscramble these four Jumbles, one letter to
each square, to form four ordinary words.

NOPIA

KELLN

GUMMAN

NARIFA

We'll set up by the lake
and wait for the geese

IMPORTANT TO
HAVE WHEN YOU
GO HUNTING.

Now arrange the circled letters to form the
surprise answer, as suggested by the above
cartoon.

Print answer   A "⬡⬡⬡⬡⬡"   ⬡⬡⬡⬡
here

JUMBLE®

Unscramble these four Jumbles, one letter to
each square, to form four ordinary words.

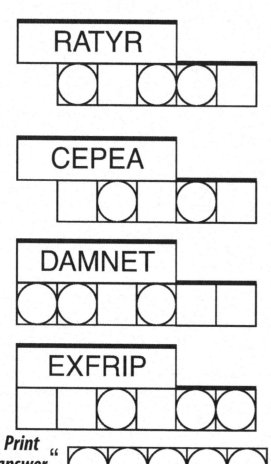

RATYR

CEPEA

DAMNET

EXFRIP

There I am,
right in front

WHAT THE FILM
STUDENT RECEIVED
WHEN HE APPEARED
IN THE MOVIE.

Now arrange the circled letters to form the
surprise answer, as suggested by the above
cartoon.

Print
answer
here

JUMBLE®

Unscramble these four Jumbles, one letter to each square, to form four ordinary words.

POSOW

GUBYL

TORBED

BALTIR

Broth with onion, that's all there is

WHAT THE FARM FAMILY ENDED UP WITH DURING THE DROUGHT.

Now arrange the circled letters to form the surprise answer, as suggested by the above cartoon.

Print answer here A ⬜⬜⬜⬜⬜ ⬜⬜⬜⬜⬜

JUMBLE®

Unscramble these four Jumbles, one letter to each square, to form four ordinary words.

RAPAT

VELED

FLOAWL

BARKEY

Oops, too much

WHEN THE BANKER'S GLASS OF BEER SPILLED OVER, THE BARTENDER SAID IT WAS AN ---

Now arrange the circled letters to form the surprise answer, as suggested by the above cartoon.

Print answer here ◯◯◯◯◯ " ◯◯◯◯◯◯ "

JUMBLE

Unscramble these four Jumbles, one letter to each square, to form four ordinary words.

PLYSH

ODITI

INSHIF

GICART

WHAT THE
GABBY BARBER DID.

Now arrange the circled letters to form the surprise answer, as suggested by the above cartoon.

Print answer here

IN " "

JUMBLE®

Unscramble these four Jumbles, one letter to
each square, to form four ordinary words.

OCTEM

REPPA

ITHELB

SLUIBY

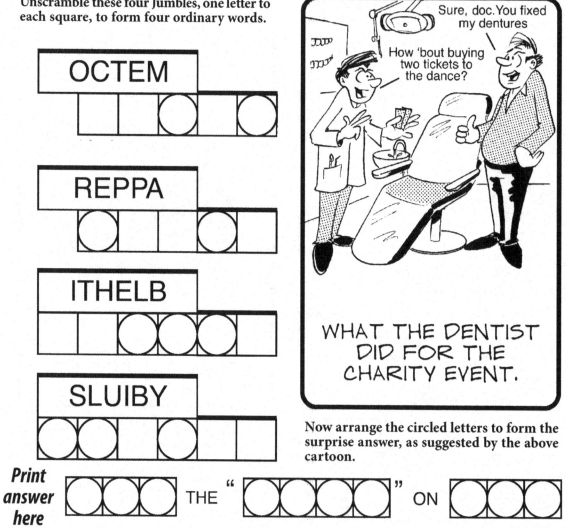

Sure, doc. You fixed
my dentures

How 'bout buying
two tickets to
the dance?

WHAT THE DENTIST
DID FOR THE
CHARITY EVENT.

Now arrange the circled letters to form the
surprise answer, as suggested by the above
cartoon.

Print
answer
here ⬚⬚⬚ THE " ⬚⬚⬚⬚ " ON ⬚⬚⬚

JUMBLE®

Unscramble these four Jumbles, one letter to each square, to form four ordinary words.

LANVA

ENUQE

BLOSMY

LAUTRI

Glad we got weekend passes

It's such a pretty time of the year

WHAT THE MILITARY COUPLE NEEDED TO SEE THE FALL COLORS.

Now arrange the circled letters to form the surprise answer, as suggested by the above cartoon.

Print answer here

 "  "

JUMBLE®

Unscramble these four Jumbles, one letter to
each square, to form four ordinary words.

TYTIK

DYNBA

CRAGIL

DIPALL

Need a refill, Suzy

Me too, darlin'

Same thing
all the time

SHE QUIT
WORKING AT THE
COFFEE SHOP
BECAUSE OF THE ---

Now arrange the circled letters to form the
surprise answer, as suggested by the above
cartoon.

**Print answer
here** ◯◯◯◯◯ " ◯◯◯◯◯ "

JUMBLE®

Unscramble these four Jumbles, one letter to each square, to form four ordinary words.

LYMAN

AKARP

PHORTY

TANSEF

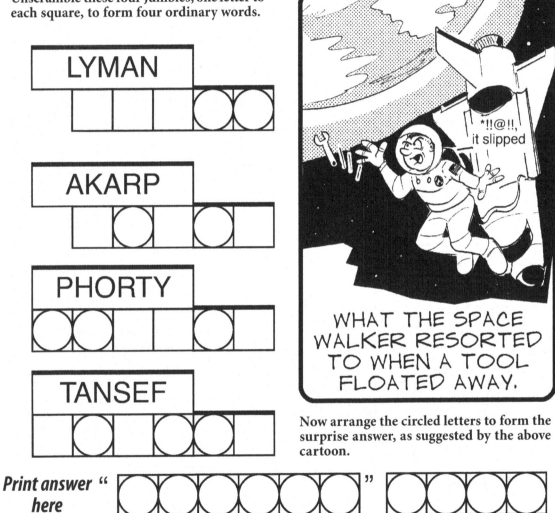

*!!@!!, it slipped

WHAT THE SPACE WALKER RESORTED TO WHEN A TOOL FLOATED AWAY.

Now arrange the circled letters to form the surprise answer, as suggested by the above cartoon.

Print answer " ⬡⬡⬡⬡⬡⬡ " ⬡⬡⬡⬡
here

61

JUMBLE®

Unscramble these four Jumbles, one letter to
each square, to form four ordinary words.

EAZUG

RYVEN

TESHEE

KUTBEC

Who's that girl looking at me?

SHE DREW THE
BRAINY STUDENT'S
ATTENTION WITH THIS.

Now arrange the circled letters to form the
surprise answer, as suggested by the above
cartoon.

Print answer here

JUMBLE®

Unscramble these four Jumbles, one letter to each square, to form four ordinary words.

CATUE

LINTE

POEQUA

VERYUP

Hee hee, I've got a straight

Full House!

WHEN THE WITCHES PLAYED POKER, THEY HAD ---

Now arrange the circled letters to form the surprise answer, as suggested by the above cartoon.

Print answer here ◯◯◯◯◯ A " ◯◯◯ "

JUMBLE®

Unscramble these four Jumbles, one letter to
each square, to form four ordinary words.

SHOIT

GHUDO

SLEPEN

ENGRYT

Who's
he?

He must be
with the band

HOW THE TRUMPET
PLAYER MANAGED TO
JOIN THE EXCLUSIVE
GATHERING.

Now arrange the circled letters to form the
surprise answer, as suggested by the above
cartoon.

Print answer
here   HE "〇〇〇〇〇〇" 〇〇

JUMBLE

Unscramble these four Jumbles, one letter to each square, to form four ordinary words.

DARRO

USTIE

ENSHOC

SHORCC

Watch out for the mailbox

Oops

WHEN DAD GAVE HIS TEENAGER A DRIVING LESSON, IT TURNED INTO---

Now arrange the circled letters to form the surprise answer, as suggested by the above cartoon.

Print answer A here " ◯◯◯◯◯ " ◯◯◯◯◯◯

JUMBLE®

Unscramble these four Jumbles, one letter to
each square, to form four ordinary words.

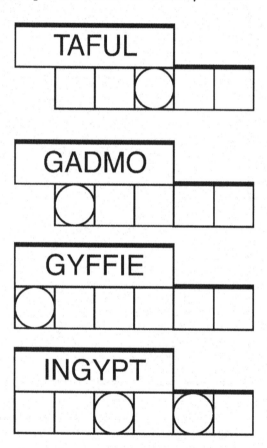

TAFUL

GADMO

GYFFIE

INGYPT

Hey, Bob.
Is that
you?

HOW A SKI TRIP
CAN END UP.

Now arrange the circled letters to form the
surprise answer, as suggested by the above
cartoon.

Print answer here

JUMBLE®

Unscramble these four Jumbles, one letter to each square, to form four ordinary words.

ZUZYF

DEACK

YUIRPT

MULASY

She's gorgeous

She doesn't sign autographs

WILCO

IMPORTANT FOR A PINUP GIRL TO BE THIS.

Now arrange the circled letters to form the surprise answer, as suggested by the above cartoon.

Print answer here

JUMBLE®

Unscramble these four Jumbles, one letter to
each square, to form four ordinary words.

ORDOB

NAGGI

DIBORM

CHARNB

He knows
everything

That's a speckled
freckle beak

ANOTHER NAME FOR
AN ORNITHOLOGIST.

Now arrange the circled letters to form the
surprise answer, as suggested by the above
cartoon.

Print
answer
here
A "⬡⬡⬡⬡⬡ ⬡⬡⬡⬡⬡⬡"

JUMBLE®

Unscramble these four Jumbles, one letter to each square, to form four ordinary words.

WENOM

PRUET

ENGINS

MOCINE

This one won't lose a second

It runs slow

HE TRADED IN HIS WATCH BECAUSE IT WAS ---

Now arrange the circled letters to form the surprise answer, as suggested by the above cartoon.

Print answer here " ◯◯◯◯ " FOR A ◯◯◯ ◯◯◯

JUMBLE®

Unscramble these four Jumbles, one letter to
each square, to form four ordinary words.

ROMUN

THRAW

POLUCE

DRENER

I'm drenched

It feels like
we're under a
waterfall

WHEN THE CAMPERS
GOT CAUGHT IN A
HEAVY CLOUDBURST,
IT FELT LIKE A – – –

Now arrange the circled letters to form the
surprise answer, as suggested by the above
cartoon.

Print answer here A " ⬡⬡⬡⬡⬡ " ⬡⬡⬡⬡

JUMBLE®

Unscramble these four Jumbles, one letter to each square, to form four ordinary words.

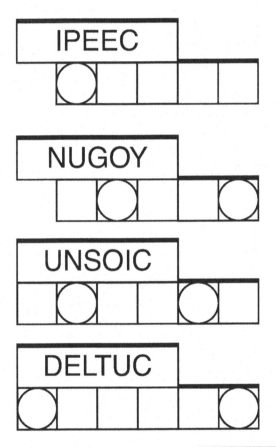

IPEEC

NUGOY

UNSOIC

DELTUC

XYZ corporation should go up $20

Anything else, gentlemen?

This is for you, Tony

WHAT THE STOCK-BROKERS GAVE THE ATTENTIVE WAITER.

Now arrange the circled letters to form the surprise answer, as suggested by the above cartoon.

Print answer here A ⬡⬡⬡⬡ " ⬡⬡⬡ "

JUMBLE®

Unscramble these four Jumbles, one letter to
each square, to form four ordinary words.

OXUMB

ZOPAT

LEBALT

MYPLOC

First, slide the
diaper under him

THE NEW PARENTS
LEARNED HOW TO
TAKE CARE OF THE
BABY FROM THE ---

Now arrange the circled letters to form the
surprise answer, as suggested by the above
cartoon.

Print answer here

JUMBLE®

Unscramble these four Jumbles, one letter to each square, to form four ordinary words.

NEPEC

DATUC

UNDIPT

HONUKO

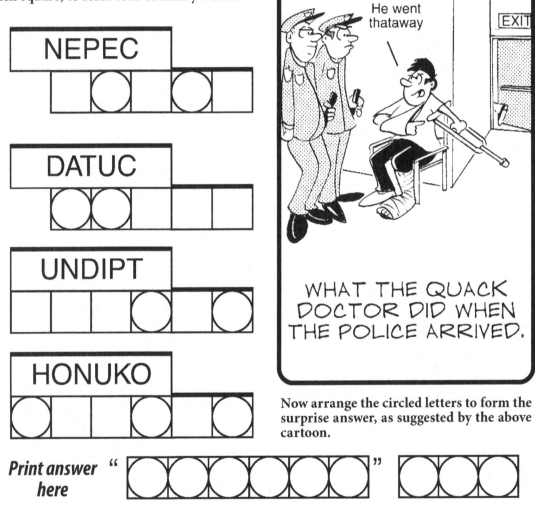

He went
thataway

EXIT

WHAT THE QUACK
DOCTOR DID WHEN
THE POLICE ARRIVED.

Now arrange the circled letters to form the surprise answer, as suggested by the above cartoon.

Print answer here "⬡⬡⬡⬡⬡⬡" ⬡⬡⬡

JUMBLE®

Unscramble these four Jumbles, one letter to each square, to form four ordinary words.

YAWNT

GEEBI

YAHRLD

CROOPE

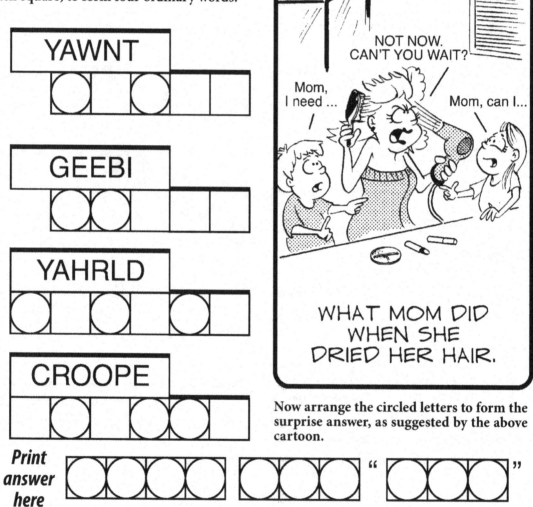

NOT NOW. CAN'T YOU WAIT?

Mom, I need ...

Mom, can I...

WHAT MOM DID WHEN SHE DRIED HER HAIR.

Now arrange the circled letters to form the surprise answer, as suggested by the above cartoon.

Print answer here

[ ][ ][ ][ ] [ ][ ][ ] " [ ][ ][ ] "

JUMBLE®

Unscramble these four Jumbles, one letter to each square, to form four ordinary words.

ANIFT

KOYLE

MAIWDY

MUJERP

I think it's fried

It won't respond

WHEN A COMPUTER FAILS, IT CAN BE ---

Now arrange the circled letters to form the surprise answer, as suggested by the above cartoon.

Print answer here " ◯◯◯◯◯◯◯◯◯ "

JUMBLE®

Unscramble these four Jumbles, one letter to each square, to form four ordinary words.

LAWRB

EFING

MUDINS

PAMEND

All we need is an ocean breeze
...and the ocean

WHEN THE COUPLE COULDN'T AFFORD A VACATION, THEY LET THEIR ---

Now arrange the circled letters to form the surprise answer, as suggested by the above cartoon.

Print answer here

"   "

JUMBLE®

Unscramble these four Jumbles, one letter to
each square, to form four ordinary words.

HANEY

FAFTY

TEELEY

GAFINC

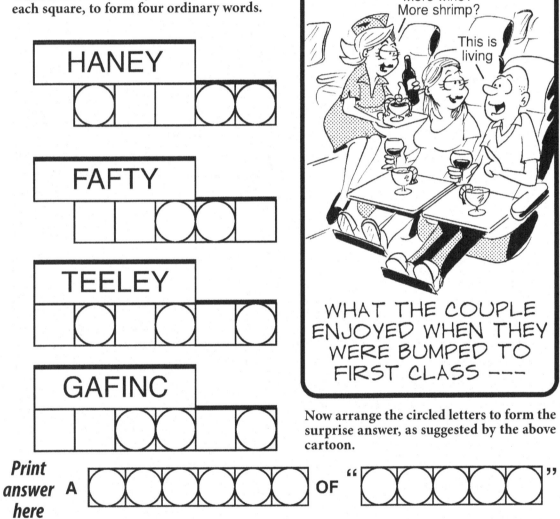

More wine?
More shrimp?

This is living

WHAT THE COUPLE
ENJOYED WHEN THEY
WERE BUMPED TO
FIRST CLASS ---

Now arrange the circled letters to form the
surprise answer, as suggested by the above
cartoon.

Print answer here

A ☐☐☐☐☐☐ OF "☐☐☐☐☐"

JUMBLE®

Unscramble these four Jumbles, one letter to each square, to form four ordinary words.

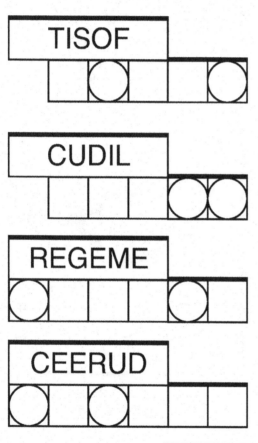

TISOF

CUDIL

REGEME

CEERUD

C'mon. Pick it up. Let's Go!

I'm ready to drop

HOW THE TEAM FELT WHEN THEIR COACH GROWLED AT THEM ALL DAY.

Now arrange the circled letters to form the surprise answer, as suggested by the above cartoon.

Print answer here

JUMBLE®

Unscramble these four Jumbles, one letter to each square, to form four ordinary words.

MILTI

TIDOT

LAFFEB

YESWIL

How did this happen?

Years of beers

WHAT HER AGING HUSBAND FACED WHEN HE DECIDED TO DIET.

Now arrange the circled letters to form the surprise answer, as suggested by the above cartoon.

Print answer here A " ◯◯◯◯◯ " OF ◯◯◯◯

JUMBLE®

Unscramble these four Jumbles, one letter to each square, to form four ordinary words.

KOYSM

VILEN

CEADDE

ENFRYZ

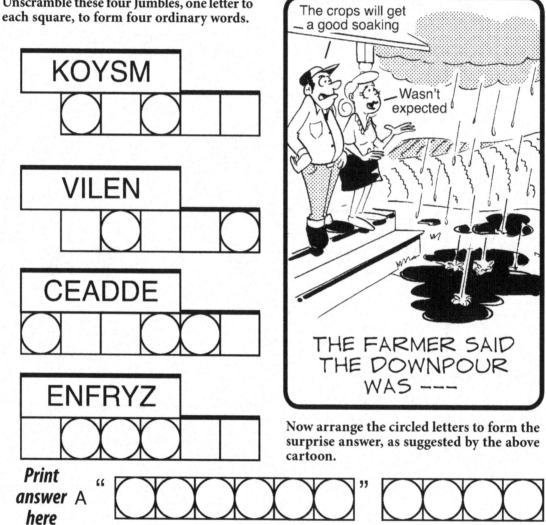

The crops will get a good soaking

Wasn't expected

THE FARMER SAID THE DOWNPOUR WAS ---

Now arrange the circled letters to form the surprise answer, as suggested by the above cartoon.

Print answer A here   " ⭘⭘⭘⭘⭘⭘ " ⭘⭘⭘⭘

JUMBLE®

Unscramble these four Jumbles, one letter to
each square, to form four ordinary words.

KOBOR

NOYME

YAMFIL

DREHWS

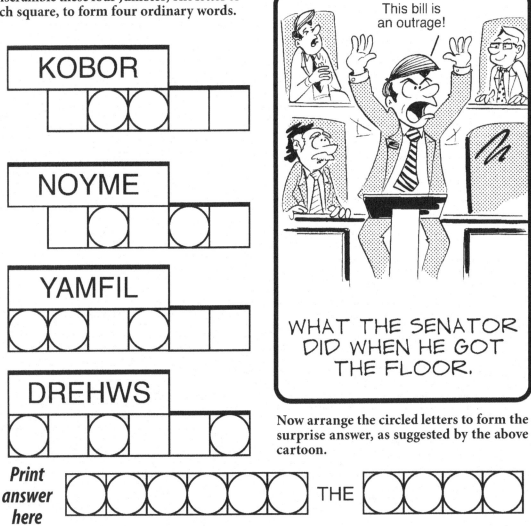

This bill is
an outrage!

WHAT THE SENATOR
DID WHEN HE GOT
THE FLOOR.

Now arrange the circled letters to form the
surprise answer, as suggested by the above
cartoon.

**Print
answer
here**

⬡⬡⬡⬡⬡⬡ THE ⬡⬡⬡⬡

81

JUMBLE®

Unscramble these four Jumbles, one letter to each square, to form four ordinary words.

SKUDY

ORRGI

ROTRAM

KALCAJ

That made him famous

WHEN THE GEOLOGIST MADE AN IMPORTANT DISCOVERY, HE BECAME A ---

Now arrange the circled letters to form the surprise answer, as suggested by the above cartoon.

Print answer here " ◯◯◯◯◯ " ◯◯◯◯

JUMBLE®

Unscramble these four Jumbles, one letter to
each square, to form four ordinary words.

INGGO

GHILT

REDUSS

REALOP

ONE WAY TO SOLVE
A KNOTTY PROBLEM.

Now arrange the circled letters to form the
surprise answer, as suggested by the above
cartoon.

**Print
answer
here**

JUMBLE®

Unscramble these four Jumbles, one letter to each square, to form four ordinary words.

PURUS

PAPYL

DEWROP

HELBED

That's lovely

I enjoy my work

WHAT THE CLERK GOT WHEN SHE DECORATED THE GIFT PACKAGE.

Now arrange the circled letters to form the surprise answer, as suggested by the above cartoon.

Print answer here " ◯◯◯◯◯◯◯ " ◯◯◯ IN IT

JUMBLE®

Unscramble these four Jumbles, one letter to each square, to form four ordinary words.

FYLOT

PIDEB

WORDSY

RENARB

Any minute, sir
It's been more than an hour

WHEN SERVICE WAS SLOW, THE HUNGRY DINERS BECAME ---

Now arrange the circled letters to form the surprise answer, as suggested by the above cartoon.

Print answer here "  "

85

JUMBLE®

Unscramble these four Jumbles, one letter to
each square, to form four ordinary words.

MYALD

BLONE

DOAZIC

PINGAY

How many times
have I told you...
Go to your room!

WHEN HE CAUGHT
JUNIOR PLAYING
WITH MATCHES,
DAD WAS ---

Now arrange the circled letters to form the
surprise answer, as suggested by the above
cartoon.

Print answer
here

JUMBLE®

Unscramble these four Jumbles, one letter to each square, to form four ordinary words.

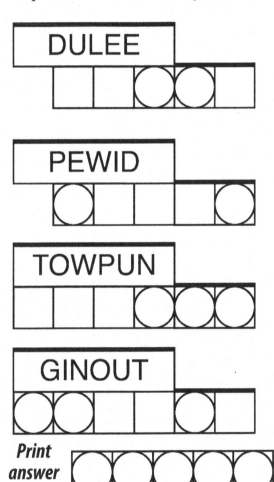

DULEE

PEWID

TOWPUN

GINOUT

This will keep it clean

WHAT MOM DID WHEN HER SON CUT HIS HAND.

Now arrange the circled letters to form the surprise answer, as suggested by the above cartoon.

Print answer here

THE

87

JUMBLE®

Unscramble these four Jumbles, one letter to
each square, to form four ordinary words.

OUDES

YAIDS

PHISBO

NECCAT

It's a big
payday

70 to 1.
You bet on
that nag?

WHEN THE RAILBIRD
BET ON THE
LONG SHOT,
IT WAS AN ----

Now arrange the circled letters to form the
surprise answer, as suggested by the above
cartoon.

Print
answer
here

"   "

JUMBLE®

Unscramble these four Jumbles, one letter to each square, to form four ordinary words.

ZAREC

YURUS

GEJLUG

DILBOE

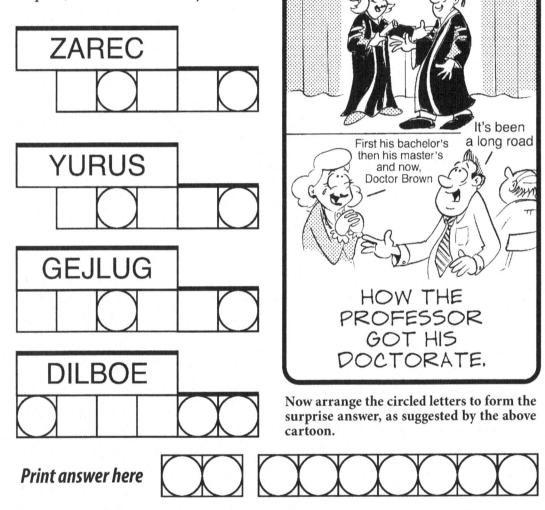

First his bachelor's then his master's and now, Doctor Brown

It's been a long road

HOW THE PROFESSOR GOT HIS DOCTORATE.

Now arrange the circled letters to form the surprise answer, as suggested by the above cartoon.

Print answer here

JUMBLE

Unscramble these four Jumbles, one letter to each square, to form four ordinary words.

HORAC

NUIFY

MOAPED

GISTED

What about ...

Maybe if we ...

We need something to tie them together

WHAT THE STRANDED BOATERS CAME UP WITH TO GET OFF THE ISLAND.

Now arrange the circled letters to form the surprise answer, as suggested by the above cartoon.

Print answer here A "⬡⬡⬡⬡" OF ⬡⬡⬡⬡⬡

JUMBLE

Unscramble these four Jumbles, one letter to each square, to form four ordinary words.

SHAMC

JABON

ENPOLL

YAUBET

I'm always on my toes

THE ZOOKEEPER DESCRIBED CLEANING THE LION CAGE AS ---

Now arrange the circled letters to form the surprise answer, as suggested by the above cartoon.

Print
answer
here
A " ⬡⬡⬡⬡⬡⬡⬡ " ⬡⬡⬡

JUMBLE®

Unscramble these four Jumbles, one letter to
each square, to form four ordinary words.

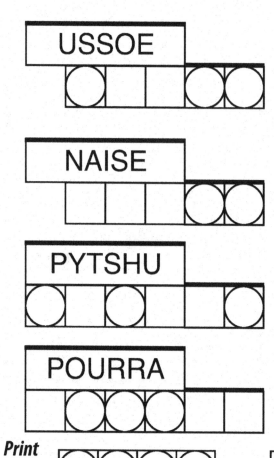

USSOE

NAISE

PYTSHU

POURRA

I'm from
XXY News.
Is it true
that ...

WHAT THE
COUNTERFEITER
SAID WHEN HE WAS
CONFRONTED BY
THE REPORTER.

Now arrange the circled letters to form the
surprise answer, as suggested by the above
cartoon.

**Print
answer
here** ⟶ THE

JUMBLE®

Unscramble these four Jumbles, one letter to each square, to form four ordinary words.

DUGAY

PHOWO

FARITY

GUNJEL

My ears hurt

He never stops

THE COUPLE LEFT THE RESTAURANT BECAUSE THE ACCORDION MUSIC WAS ---

Now arrange the circled letters to form the surprise answer, as suggested by the above cartoon.

Print answer here " ◯◯◯◯◯ " ◯◯◯

JUMBLE®

Unscramble these four Jumbles, one letter to
each square, to form four ordinary words.

LOVEH

SIVOR

LUBOSE

TENCED

Some of it,
I think

Did you
get it?

WHAT THE COUPLE
SAID WHEN THE
POETRY READING
LEFT THEM PUZZLED.

Now arrange the circled letters to form the
surprise answer, as suggested by the above
cartoon.

*Print
answer
here*

BE "⬡⬡⬡⬡⬡"

JUMBLE®

Unscramble these four Jumbles, one letter to each square, to form four ordinary words.

LERED

REGUP

ICETOX

INCLEP

Can we get a room?

Read the sign

NO VACANCY

WHEN THEY ASKED FOR A ROOM, THE HOTEL CLERK WAS ---

Now arrange the circled letters to form the surprise answer, as suggested by the above cartoon.

Print answer here

JUMBLE®

Unscramble these four Jumbles, one letter to each square, to form four ordinary words.

TOJUS

CANYF

PAFFOY

SUNDOL

I'm loading up on carbs

That's a lot of food

MINI-MART

POI

WHAT THE RUNNER ATE BEFORE THE BIG RACE.

Now arrange the circled letters to form the surprise answer, as suggested by the above cartoon.

Print answer here " ⬚⬚⬚⬚ " ⬚⬚⬚⬚

96

JUMBLE®

Unscramble these four Jumbles, one letter to each square, to form four ordinary words.

EYAPE

IDDEC

PEESLY

VOALAW

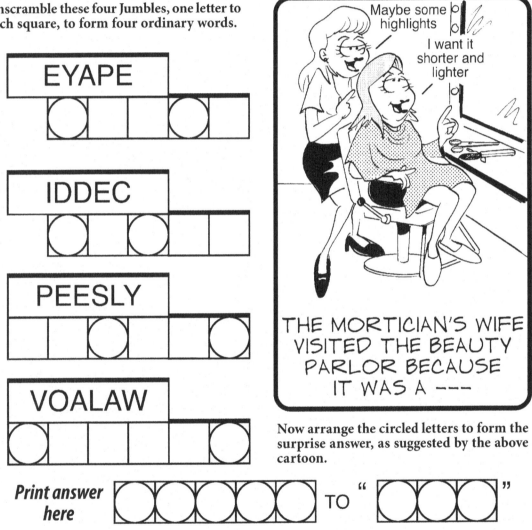

Maybe some highlights

I want it shorter and lighter

THE MORTICIAN'S WIFE VISITED THE BEAUTY PARLOR BECAUSE IT WAS A ---

Now arrange the circled letters to form the surprise answer, as suggested by the above cartoon.

Print answer here ◯◯◯◯◯ TO " ◯◯◯ "

JUMBLE®

Unscramble these four Jumbles, one letter to each square, to form four ordinary words.

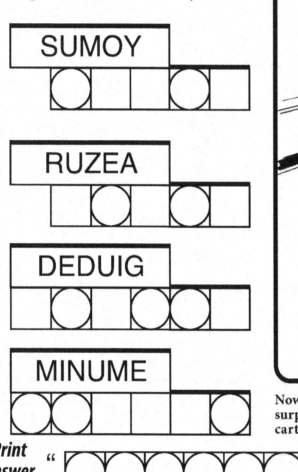

SUMOY

RUZEA

DEDUIG

MINUME

Your Vacation. I went to the beach, swam, and visited my grandparents. End of story.

WHEN THE PUPIL TOLD THE CLASS WHAT HE DID ON VACATION, HE ---

Now arrange the circled letters to form the surprise answer, as suggested by the above cartoon.

Print answer here "◯◯◯◯◯◯◯-◯◯◯◯" IT

JUMBLE®

Unscramble these four Jumbles, one letter to each square, to form four ordinary words.

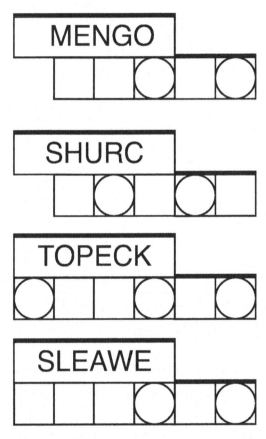

MENGO

SHURC

TOPECK

SLEAWE

Freshly brewed. Want a refill?

Always busy, good tips and benefits

WHAT THEY GOT WHEN THEY WORKED IN THE COFFEE SHOP.

Now arrange the circled letters to form the surprise answer, as suggested by the above cartoon.

Print answer here

 OF "  "

JUMBLE®

Unscramble these four Jumbles, one letter to
each square, to form four ordinary words.

MOPET

ASAIL

MASHNO

YEWARL

I'll fix it
tomorrow

You said
that
yesterday

WHEN HE DIDN'T FIX
THE LEAK, HIS WIFE
SAID IT WAS A ---

Now arrange the circled letters to form the
surprise answer, as suggested by the above
cartoon.

**Print
answer
here**

"   "

JUMBLE

Unscramble these four Jumbles, one letter to each square, to form four ordinary words.

SHWIK

GEMAL

ASTOAN

PUMACS

Come on over and jump in

EASY TO DO WITH YOUR NEIGHBORS WHEN YOU BUILD A SWIMMING POOL.

Now arrange the circled letters to form the surprise answer, as suggested by the above cartoon.

Print answer here

A " "

JUMBLE®

Unscramble these four Jumbles, one letter to each square, to form four ordinary words.

FORLO

TCHAB

FLYNUK

NAEVLE

All that soot. I'm always coughing

WHAT THE CHIMNEY SWEEP HAD TO DEAL WITH.

Now arrange the circled letters to form the surprise answer, as suggested by the above cartoon.

Print answer here ☐☐☐ " ☐☐☐☐ "

JUMBLE

Unscramble these four Jumbles, one letter to each square, to form four ordinary words.

JYTET

POSOT

NINTTE

SNOPER

What a sale. I'm beat.

WHAT HIS WIFE DID AND WAS WHEN SHE SHOPPED ALL DAY.

Now arrange the circled letters to form the surprise answer, as suggested by the above cartoon.

Print answer here

 AND

103

JUMBLE®

Unscramble these four Jumbles, one letter to
each square, to form four ordinary words.

MYAIT

NEMIR

RAWHOR

WAHGIE

I have
one more
in the
bull's eye

THE ARCHERY
COMPETITION WAS
WON BY AN ---

Now arrange the circled letters to form the
surprise answer, as suggested by the above
cartoon.

Print
answer
here

JUMBLE®

Unscramble these four Jumbles, one letter to
each square, to form four ordinary words.

ESTUG

THONC

VIPSEL

KLAYEC

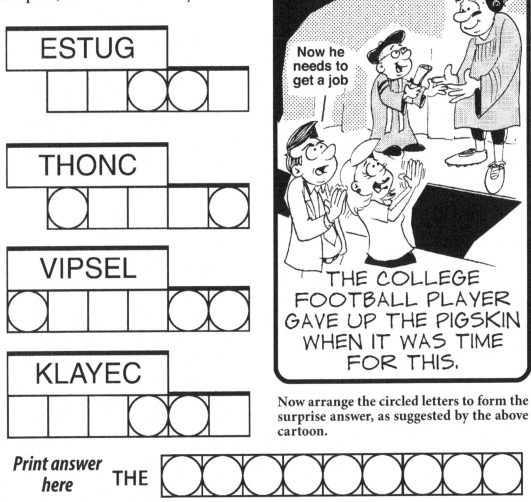

Now he needs to get a job

THE COLLEGE
FOOTBALL PLAYER
GAVE UP THE PIGSKIN
WHEN IT WAS TIME
FOR THIS.

Now arrange the circled letters to form the
surprise answer, as suggested by the above
cartoon.

Print answer
here   THE ◯◯◯◯◯◯◯◯◯◯

JUMBLE®

Unscramble these four Jumbles, one letter to each square, to form four ordinary words.

ANCKK

PYDET

LUMEFF

YIPLOC

You're doing a fine job, Sam

404

WHY THE BOOKKEEPER RECEIVED A RAISE.

Now arrange the circled letters to form the surprise answer, as suggested by the above cartoon.

Print answer here   HE " ◯◯◯◯◯◯◯ "

JUMBLE®

Unscramble these four Jumbles, one letter to each square, to form four ordinary words.

KNUSK

WAKTE

LAGBOM

INDOAJ

Ask me anything

I'm new. Where's the doctor's lounge?

INFORMATION

THE PLASTIC SURGEON SOUGHT THE CLERK'S HELP BECAUSE SHE HAD A ---

Now arrange the circled letters to form the surprise answer, as suggested by the above cartoon.

Print answer here " ◯◯◯◯◯◯ " ◯◯◯

JUMBLE®

Unscramble these four Jumbles, one letter to
each square, to form four ordinary words.

ALOCK

GUNST

CROUTY

COBDIE

He put a charge
in that one

THE ELECTRICIAN
JOINED THE BASEBALL
TEAM BECAUSE HE ---

Now arrange the circled letters to form the
surprise answer, as suggested by the above
cartoon.

Print
answer
here

" "

JUMBLE®

Unscramble these four Jumbles, one letter to each square, to form four ordinary words.

TADPA

ASTUE

LALCOW

ENBOGE

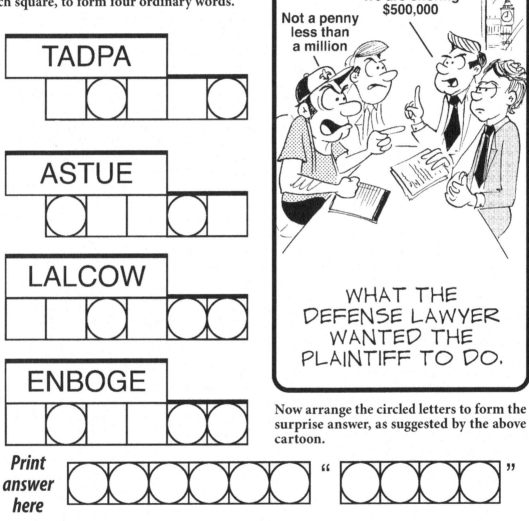

We are offering $500,000

Not a penny less than a million

WHAT THE DEFENSE LAWYER WANTED THE PLAINTIFF TO DO.

Now arrange the circled letters to form the surprise answer, as suggested by the above cartoon.

Print answer here

" "

JUMBLE®

Unscramble these four Jumbles, one letter to
each square, to form four ordinary words.

ENWIC

LURTY

ZARLID

YAWALY

We have so
much to learn
about them

THEY WERE
MOTIVATED TO HUNT
FOR SNAKES
BY THE ---

Now arrange the circled letters to form the
surprise answer, as suggested by the above
cartoon.

Print
answer
here "〇〇〇〇〇" OF THE 〇〇〇〇

JUMBLE®

Unscramble these four Jumbles, one letter to each square, to form four ordinary words.

RUYLB

TINFE

PHULED

GAIMBY

Sorry, everyone. My fault

It takes a big man to admit an error

WHEN THE FOREMAN SAID HE WAS ALL WRONG, THE WORKERS SAID HE WAS ---

Now arrange the circled letters to form the surprise answer, as suggested by the above cartoon.

Print answer here ◯◯◯ ◯◯◯◯◯◯

JUMBLE®

Unscramble these four Jumbles, one letter to
each square, to form four ordinary words.

ROWBE

MEZIA

REMMOY

GRACIT

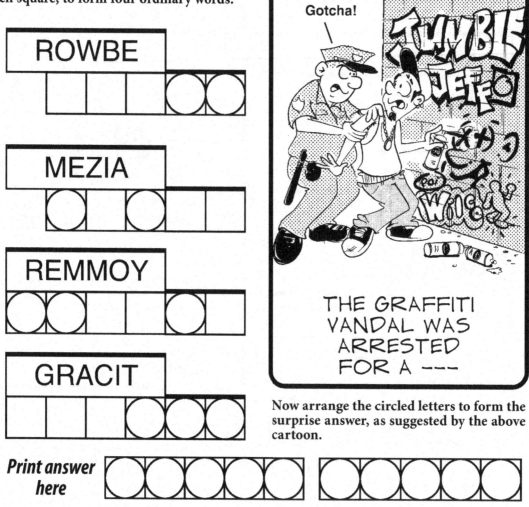

Gotcha!

THE GRAFFITI
VANDAL WAS
ARRESTED
FOR A ---

Now arrange the circled letters to form the
surprise answer, as suggested by the above
cartoon.

**Print answer
here**

JUMBLE®

Unscramble these four Jumbles, one letter to each square, to form four ordinary words.

NUDAT

WOSOP

GABLEE

SATTEE

Time to go home. See you tomorrow, Joe

WHAT THE NIGHT OWL DID DAY AFTER DAY.

Now arrange the circled letters to form the surprise answer, as suggested by the above cartoon.

Print answer here ⬡⬡⬡⬡ TO ⬡⬡⬡⬡⬡

113

PUZZLE 111

JUMBLE®

Unscramble these four Jumbles, one letter to each square, to form four ordinary words.

SHOWE

BAXOR

MUBHEL

HIGLES

I'm getting some great footage for my program

SHOT BY THE TELEVISION HOST ON THE SAFARI.

Now arrange the circled letters to form the surprise answer, as suggested by the above cartoon.

Print answer here A " ◯◯◯◯ " ◯◯◯◯

JUMBLE®

Unscramble these four Jumbles, one letter to each square, to form four ordinary words.

SURNP

EFTUL

PAWNEO

VOICEN

Your change, sir, and thank you!

EASY TO TURN A FIFTY INTO.

Now arrange the circled letters to form the surprise answer, as suggested by the above cartoon.

Print answer here A ○○○ AND ○○○ ○○○○○

JUMBLE

Unscramble these four Jumbles, one letter to each square, to form four ordinary words.

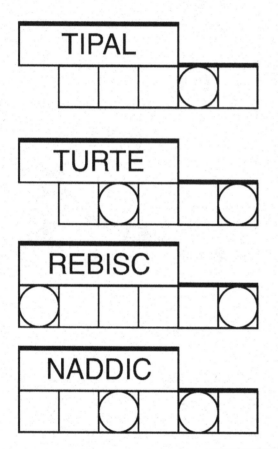

TIPAL

TURTE

REBISC

NADDIC

I can't believe they beat us

This was our big chance

WHEN THEIR TEAM LOST THE BIG GAME, THE HOME CROWD WAS ---

Now arrange the circled letters to form the surprise answer, as suggested by the above cartoon.

Print answer here

JUMBLE®

Unscramble these four Jumbles, one letter to
each square, to form four ordinary words.

POUCE

KANET

TAPECK

LORMAN

You're a liar!
I'll knock
your block off!

Now, boys,
settle down

WHAT THE BARTENDER
DID WHEN THE
DISAGREEMENT GOT
HEATED.

Now arrange the circled letters to form the
surprise answer, as suggested by the above
cartoon.

**Print answer
here** ⬡⬡⬡⬡ HIS ⬡⬡⬡⬡

117

JUMBLE

Unscramble these four Jumbles, one letter to each square, to form four ordinary words.

GYROL

DACKE

RIGLYM

LIVEEW

I need a change. I'm going to travel for a while

Sounds like you've soured on the job

WHY THE PICKLE MAKER DECIDED TO QUIT.

Now arrange the circled letters to form the surprise answer, as suggested by the above cartoon.

Print answer here   IT WAS   " ⃝⃝⃝⃝⃝ "   ⃝⃝⃝⃝

118

JUMBLE®

Unscramble these four Jumbles, one letter to
each square, to form four ordinary words.

DULGI

DICAR

INLARM

UNEEVA

Isn't this romantic?

I can hardly see the road

THE COUPLE WENT FOR A SPIN IN THE STORM BECAUSE IT WAS ---

Now arrange the circled letters to form the
surprise answer, as suggested by the above
cartoon.

Print answer here " ◯◯◯◯◯◯◯◯ " ◯◯◯◯

119

JUMBLE®

Unscramble these four Jumbles, one letter to each square, to form four ordinary words.

CERDY

TOORB

UNDASE

FRIEVY

SNRXXXX

Come in, AJAX. Come in

WHEN THE EXHAUSTED SPY WENT TO BED, HE WAS ---

Now arrange the circled letters to form the surprise answer, as suggested by the above cartoon.

Print answer here

JUMBLE®

Unscramble these four Jumbles, one letter to each square, to form four ordinary words.

BUIME

FLAYE

SIGAHR

GOYNEX

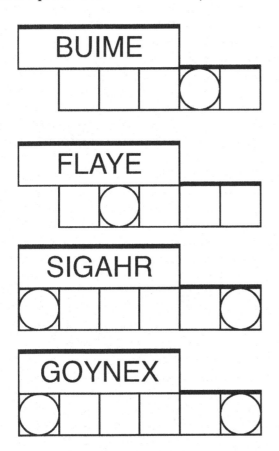

You've made my day

WHAT MOM GOT FROM "ONE HUG."

Now arrange the circled letters to form the surprise answer, as suggested by the above cartoon.

Print answer here

JUMBLE®

Unscramble these four Jumbles, one letter to
each square, to form four ordinary words.

CLUNE

DIPTE

SPUMGY

REBURB

How did he
do that?

He's a
prestidigi...
something

ANOTHER NAME
FOR A GREAT
MAGICIAN.

Now arrange the circled letters to form the
surprise answer, as suggested by the above
cartoon.

Print
answer A
here

"   "

JUMBLE®

Unscramble these four Jumbles, one letter to each square, to form four ordinary words.

TAGUM

OPTIA

GESTAK

TARRMY

You'll be back again

WHAT THE WARDEN GAVE THE REPEAT OFFENDER.

Now arrange the circled letters to form the surprise answer, as suggested by the above cartoon.

Print answer here A ◯◯◯◯ " ◯◯◯ "

JUMBLE®

Unscramble these four Jumbles, one letter to
each square, to form four ordinary words.

YONOL

BELZA

TSATLE

AGGIZZ

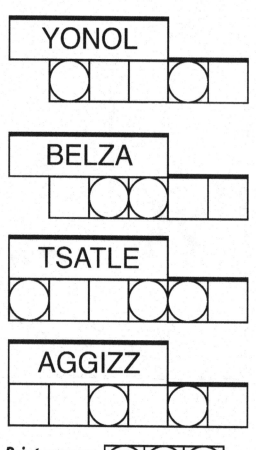

NDINGS 1-KNUREK 2-STEWARD 3-PAT

THE DRIVER WON
THE ROAD RACE
BECAUSE
HE KNEW ---

Now arrange the circled letters to form the
surprise answer, as suggested by the above
cartoon.

**Print answer
here** ⬭⬭⬭ THE ⬭⬭⬭⬭⬭⬭

JUMBLE®

Unscramble these four Jumbles, one letter to each square, to form four ordinary words.

NOAGY

BABIR

DARAPE

YAIMDS

Hello, gorgeous. Are you new here?

WHAT SHE RAN INTO AT THE WATER COOLER.

Now arrange the circled letters to form the surprise answer, as suggested by the above cartoon.

Print answer here A ◯◯◯ " ◯◯◯◯ "

JUMBLE

Unscramble these four Jumbles, one letter to
each square, to form four ordinary words.

SLURY

ADURF

BRUMEN

SHUBLE

CITY
HALL

This will
be costly

All the plows
are out

WHAT THE CITY
FATHERS USED TO
CLEAN UP AFTER THE
WINTER STORM.

Now arrange the circled letters to form the
surprise answer, as suggested by the above
cartoon.

Print answer
here   A " ◯◯◯◯◯ " ◯◯◯◯

JUMBLE®

Unscramble these four Jumbles, one letter to each square, to form four ordinary words.

LAGED

KYDUS

ABBIDE

NAHMLY

I didn't see it coming

WHEN HER CLIENT WAS ARRESTED FOR FORGERY, THE CLAIRVOYANT SAID IT WAS ---

Now arrange the circled letters to form the surprise answer, as suggested by the above cartoon.

Print answer here   A ☐◯◯◯ " ◯◯◯◯ "

JUMBLE®

Unscramble these four Jumbles, one letter to
each square, to form four ordinary words.

AVVLE

STRON

CLEBUK

RANHOP

NO CHECKS NO CREDIT

Let me see
some I.D.

WHAT THE
STOREKEEPER
WANTED FOR A KEG
OF BEER.

Now arrange the circled letters to form the
surprise answer, as suggested by the above
cartoon.

**Print
answer
here**

ON
THE

JUMBLE®

Unscramble these four Jumbles, one letter to
each square, to form four ordinary words.

PHLYS

CEENI

SPEGOL

ENCOSH

and ...where
was I?

WHAT HAPPENED TO
THE POLITICIAN WHEN
THE TELEPROMPTER
FAILED.

Now arrange the circled letters to form the
surprise answer, as suggested by the above
cartoon.

**Print
answer
here**

HE
WAS

" ◯◯◯◯◯◯◯◯◯◯◯ "

JUMBLE®

Unscramble these four Jumbles, one letter to each square, to form four ordinary words.

DOYNS

RETEX

NEPPIS

ONSWID

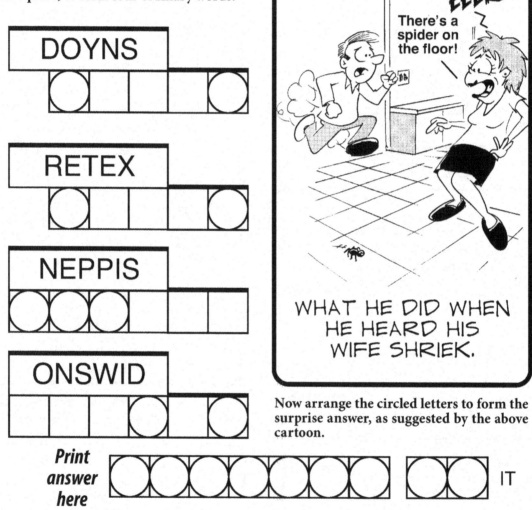

There's a spider on the floor!

EEEK!

WHAT HE DID WHEN HE HEARD HIS WIFE SHRIEK.

Now arrange the circled letters to form the surprise answer, as suggested by the above cartoon.

Print answer here

⬭⬭⬭⬭⬭⬭⬭ ⬭⬭ IT

JUMBLE®

Unscramble these four Jumbles, one letter to each square, to form four ordinary words.

VALEG

UNFYN

LOPPIN

FREIHE

Twenty more pounds. It's hard to stomach

HA HA HA HA

WHEN THE COMEDIAN GAINED WEIGHT, HE TRIED TO ---

Now arrange the circled letters to form the surprise answer, as suggested by the above cartoon.

Print answer here ⬡⬡⬡⬡⬡ IT ⬡⬡⬡

JUMBLE®

Unscramble these four Jumbles, one letter to each square, to form four ordinary words.

STULY

ENCAP

LADLAB

SCYTIK

Come to me, my little fishes

WHAT THE WITCH DID ON THE FISHING TRIP.

Now arrange the circled letters to form the surprise answer, as suggested by the above cartoon.

Print answer here " ☐☐☐☐ " A ☐☐☐☐☐☐

JUMBLE®

Unscramble these four Jumbles, one letter to each square, to form four ordinary words.

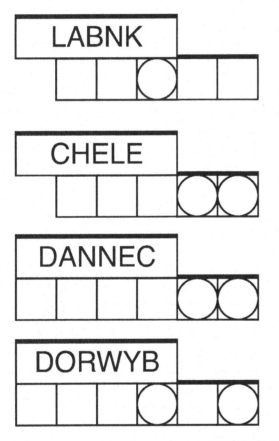

LABNK

CHELE

DANNEC

DORWYB

The fox~ COUGH COUGH is in the aahChoo! henhouse

WHEN THE SPY MADE A SECRET CALL, HE ---

Now arrange the circled letters to form the surprise answer, as suggested by the above cartoon.

Print answer here ◯◯◯ A ◯◯◯◯

JUMBLE®

Unscramble these four Jumbles, one letter to each square, to form four ordinary words.

INHEW

SBENO

XTEICE

GYLINK

Do you like it?

How much?

WHEN SHE BOUGHT
ANOTHER PILLBOX
HAT, HER HUSBAND
SAID IT WAS ----

Now arrange the circled letters to form the surprise answer, as suggested by the above cartoon.

Print answer here " ◯◯◯◯◯◯◯◯◯ "

JUMBLE®

Unscramble these four Jumbles, one letter to each square, to form four ordinary words.

DRAIP

HOPAC

KALLIA

ROBRAW

Not for me

You'll start off digging ditches

HELP WANTED

FOR SOME, AN UNPOPULAR WAY OF MAKING MONEY.

Now arrange the circled letters to form the surprise answer, as suggested by the above cartoon.

Print answer here

JUMBLE

Unscramble these four Jumbles, one letter to each square, to form four ordinary words.

MIFLY

THUCE

CUSSID

LAIVES

WHAT MOM MADE HIM DO WHEN HE WAS LATE FOR HIS PIANO LESSON.

Now arrange the circled letters to form the surprise answer, as suggested by the above cartoon.

Print answer here ⬡⬡⬡⬡ THE ⬡⬡⬡⬡⬡

JUMBLE®

Unscramble these four Jumbles, one letter to each square, to form four ordinary words.

LOFAR

ROYAF

MOYPLE

PRIMTO

Get out!

Ooops, too high

THE PANCAKE COOK WAS FIRED BECAUSE HE WAS A ---

Now arrange the circled letters to form the surprise answer, as suggested by the above cartoon.

Print answer here

JUMBLE®

Unscramble these four Jumbles, one letter to each square, to form four ordinary words.

THALC

HERIK

REENOC

CHERAB

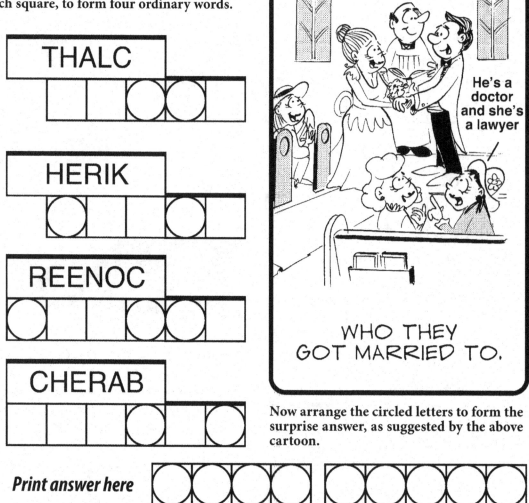

He's a doctor and she's a lawyer

WHO THEY GOT MARRIED TO.

Now arrange the circled letters to form the surprise answer, as suggested by the above cartoon.

Print answer here

JUMBLE®

Unscramble these four Jumbles, one letter to each square, to form four ordinary words.

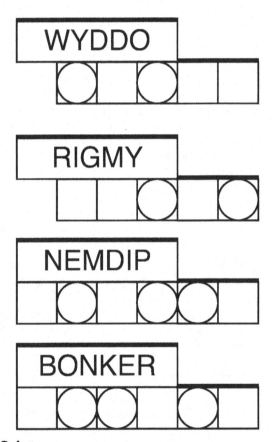

WYDDO

RIGMY

NEMDIP

BONKER

Sure. You need new cords

Can you fix these lamps?

WHAT THE DOWN-AND-OUT HANDYMAN DID WHEN HE NEEDED CASH.

Now arrange the circled letters to form the surprise answer, as suggested by the above cartoon.

Print answer here " ☐☐☐☐☐ " FOR ☐☐☐☐☐

JUMBLE®

Unscramble these four Jumbles, one letter to each square, to form four ordinary words.

TOSOY

SITOF

FRUIPY

LENZOZ

Just a little left-hand English

A GOOD STRATEGY FOR A POCKET BILLIARDS TEAM.

Now arrange the circled letters to form the surprise answer, as suggested by the above cartoon.

Print answer here " ⬡⬡⬡⬡⬡ " THEIR ⬡⬡⬡⬡⬡⬡⬡

JUMBLE®

Unscramble these four Jumbles, one letter to
each square, to form four ordinary words.

LIPTO

FERAT

DINKLY

TIFLLE

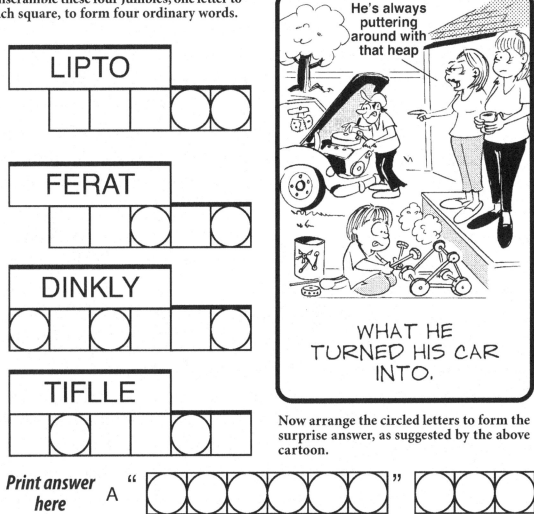

He's always
puttering
around with
that heap

WHAT HE
TURNED HIS CAR
INTO.

Now arrange the circled letters to form the
surprise answer, as suggested by the above
cartoon.

*Print answer
here* A "⬡⬡⬡⬡⬡⬡" ⬡⬡⬡

JUMBLE®

Unscramble these four Jumbles, one letter to each square, to form four ordinary words.

AMDAM

THEIG

YINJET

DIMYAD

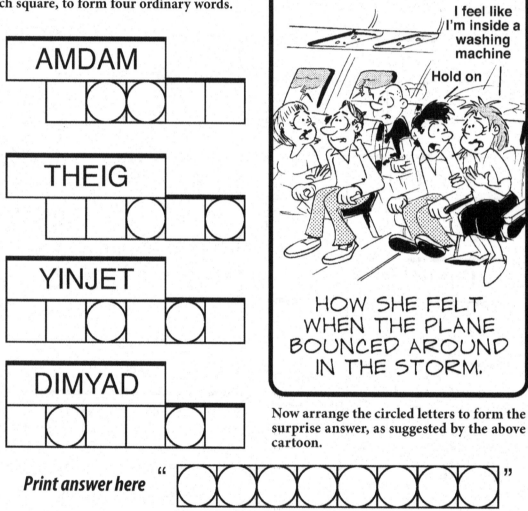

I feel like I'm inside a washing machine

Hold on

HOW SHE FELT WHEN THE PLANE BOUNCED AROUND IN THE STORM.

Now arrange the circled letters to form the surprise answer, as suggested by the above cartoon.

Print answer here " ◯◯◯◯◯◯◯◯◯ "

JUMBLE®

Unscramble these four Jumbles, one letter to each square, to form four ordinary words.

WENIT

KULFE

TRUXAS

SNAFET

I'll make it look lifelike

THE HUNTER HIRED THE TAXIDERMIST BECAUSE HE ---

Now arrange the circled letters to form the surprise answer, as suggested by the above cartoon.

Print answer here ◯◯◯◯ HIS " ◯◯◯◯◯ "

143

JUMBLE®

Unscramble these four Jumbles, one letter to each square, to form four ordinary words.

VONEY

TOISH

RAZABA

SITMIF

...jet pilot.. got my degree with honors... run ten miles a day ...

WHAT SHE EXPERIENCED ON HER DATE WITH THE EYE DOCTOR.

Now arrange the circled letters to form the surprise answer, as suggested by the above cartoon.

Print answer here " "

JUMBLE®

Unscramble these four Jumbles, one letter to
each square, to form four ordinary words.

GERME

DABNY

QUIDIL

TRARAT

Finally.
That was
a tough one

HOW HE FELT
WHEN HE UNPLUGGED
THE SINK.

Now arrange the circled letters to form the
surprise answer, as suggested by the above
cartoon.

Print answer here "  "

JUMBLE®

Unscramble these four Jumbles, one letter to
each square, to form four ordinary words.

NOSOW

PIGER

TIPPUL

NEPELS

You owe me
a favor

What do you
need?

A POLITICIAN WILL
DO THIS WHEN
FACED WITH A
KNOTTY PROBLEM.

Now arrange the circled letters to form the
surprise answer, as suggested by the above
cartoon.

**Print
answer
here**

JUMBLE®

Unscramble these four Jumbles, one letter to
each square, to form four ordinary words.

DUWNE

TRIVE

MUHLIE

TIPURY

... and then Susie
said ... blah, blah,
blah, blah ...

Are you
ready to
order?

WHAT HER FRIEND
DID TO SHORTEN
THE LONG STORY.

Now arrange the circled letters to form the
surprise answer, as suggested by the above
cartoon.

*Print
answer
here*

JUMBLE®

Unscramble these four Jumbles, one letter to each square, to form four ordinary words.

NICCY

BOMIL

PATTOE

ORPAND

The hat is bulky, but warm

THE ARCTIC EXPLORER SAID HIS HEAD GEAR WAS A – – –

Now arrange the circled letters to form the surprise answer, as suggested by the above cartoon.

Print answer here

JUMBLE

Unscramble these four Jumbles, one letter to
each square, to form four ordinary words.

DORRA

NAIPO

CLORLS

DAJEGG

Out of
my way!

After you,
sir

WHAT IT CAN TAKE
TO PUT UP WITH
BAD MANNERS.

Now arrange the circled letters to form the
surprise answer, as suggested by the above
cartoon.

Print answer here

149

JUMBLE®

Unscramble these four Jumbles, one letter to
each square, to form four ordinary words.

GEALL

NAYDD

QULLAS

INKANP

BARN DANCE

Is he
seeing
anyone?

ALTHOUGH THE
BACHELOR OWNED
A LARGE FARM, THE
GIRLS SAID HE WAS ---

Now arrange the circled letters to form the
surprise answer, as suggested by the above
cartoon.

Print answer here " ◯◯◯◯◯◯◯◯◯ "

150

JUMBLE®

Unscramble these four Jumbles, one letter to each square, to form four ordinary words.

HEWIG

ETTIL

HARMIO

REDOWP

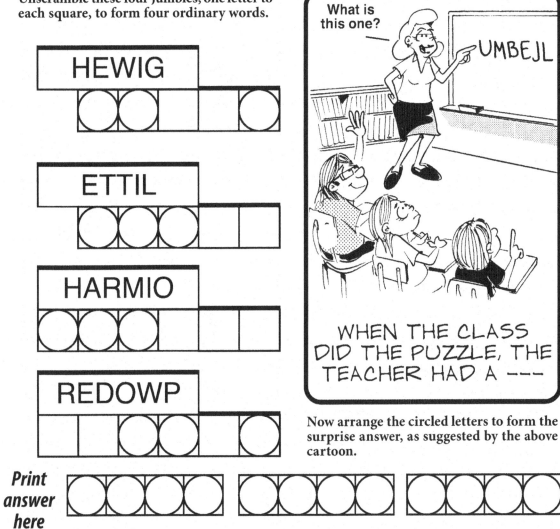

What is this one?

UMBEJL

WHEN THE CLASS DID THE PUZZLE, THE TEACHER HAD A - - -

Now arrange the circled letters to form the surprise answer, as suggested by the above cartoon.

Print answer here

JUMBLE

Unscramble these four Jumbles, one letter to
each square, to form four ordinary words.

REFIA

CROWE

LAVASS

CISTEB

That should
do it

WHAT THE DOCTOR
USED WHEN HIS
DESK CHAIR
SQUEAKED.

Now arrange the circled letters to form the
surprise answer, as suggested by the above
cartoon.

Print answer here

JUMBLE®

Unscramble these four Jumbles, one letter to
each square, to form four ordinary words.

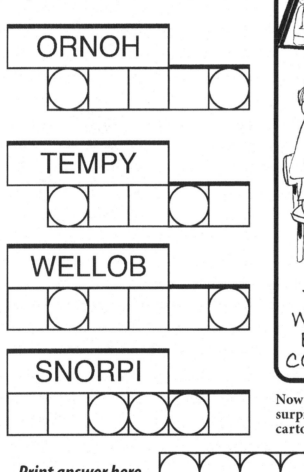

ORNOH

TEMPY

WELLOB

SNORPI

Sunny all day

THE FORECASTER
WAS WEATHER WISE,
BUT THE GOLFERS
CONSIDERED HIM ---

Now arrange the circled letters to form the
surprise answer, as suggested by the above
cartoon.

Print answer here

JUMBLE®

Unscramble these four Jumbles, one letter to each square, to form four ordinary words.

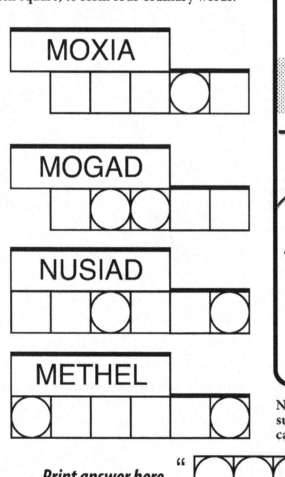

MOXIA

MOGAD

NUSIAD

METHEL

We won again!

WHAT THEY ENDED UP WITH AT THE GREYHOUND RACES.

Now arrange the circled letters to form the surprise answer, as suggested by the above cartoon.

Print answer here "◯◯◯" ◯◯◯◯

JUMBLE®

Unscramble these four Jumbles, one letter to
each square, to form four ordinary words.

SEMYS

FITEB

DOLIBY

ULSSET

He knows how to tell a story

A JOKE WILL
GET THE MOST
LAUGHS WHEN
THE ---

Now arrange the circled letters to form the
surprise answer, as suggested by the above
cartoon.

**Print answer
here**
⬡⬡⬡⬡ ⬡⬡⬡⬡⬡ IT

JUMBLE®

Unscramble these four Jumbles, one letter to
each square, to form four ordinary words.

ZIERP

PORDO

BREEMM

SCUMEL

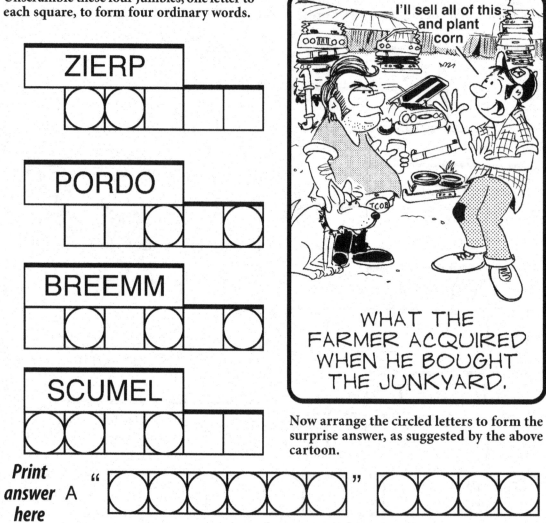

I'll sell all of this
and plant
corn

WHAT THE
FARMER ACQUIRED
WHEN HE BOUGHT
THE JUNKYARD.

Now arrange the circled letters to form the
surprise answer, as suggested by the above
cartoon.

Print
answer A   "⬡⬡⬡⬡⬡⬡⬡" ⬡⬡⬡⬡
here

JUMBLE®

Unscramble these four Jumbles, one letter to each square, to form four ordinary words.

HASUQ

RUILD

CRAHNB

UNDOAR

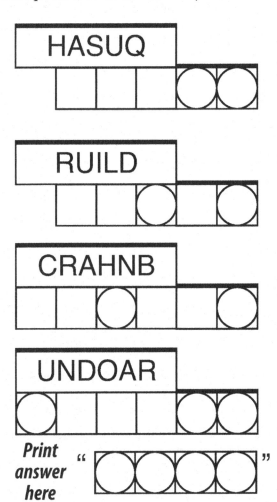

Six hours without a break. I can barely hold the file.

THE MANICURIST SAID NAILS ARE THIS.

Now arrange the circled letters to form the surprise answer, as suggested by the above cartoon.

Print answer here " ⬡⬡⬡⬡ " ON THE ⬡⬡⬡⬡⬡

JUMBLE®

Unscramble these four Jumbles, one letter to each square, to form four ordinary words.

LAURR

MOWNE

SETTEA

RETORR

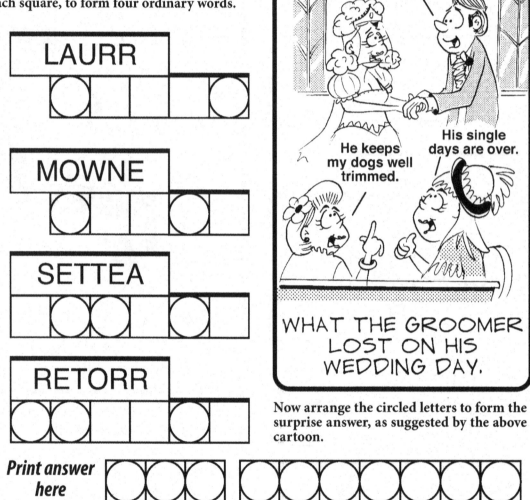

I do.

He keeps my dogs well trimmed.

His single days are over.

WHAT THE GROOMER LOST ON HIS WEDDING DAY.

Now arrange the circled letters to form the surprise answer, as suggested by the above cartoon.

Print answer here

JUMBLE®

Unscramble these four Jumbles, one letter to each square, to form four ordinary words.

AWNTY

LOOFI

THOUPS

YABSUW

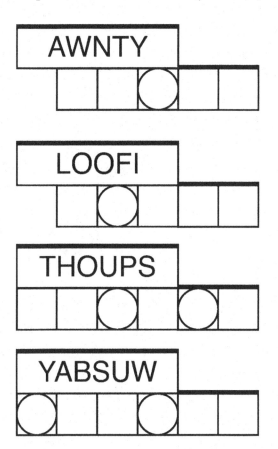

Tough work. It rained almost every day.

WHEN THE SPRING PLANTING WAS COMPLETE, THE FARMER SAID IT WAS ---

Now arrange the circled letters to form the surprise answer, as suggested by the above cartoon.

Print answer here

JUMBLE®

Unscramble these four Jumbles, one letter to each square, to form four ordinary words.

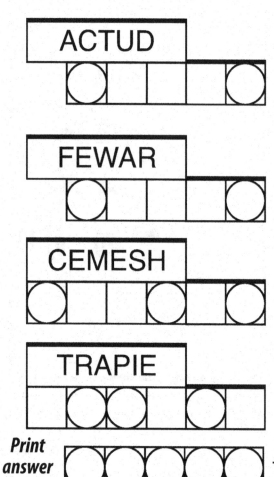

ACTUD

FEWAR

CEMESH

TRAPIE

C'mon.
We can do it!

Pull
harder!

WHAT THE PICNICKERS DID DURING THE TUG OF WAR.

Now arrange the circled letters to form the surprise answer, as suggested by the above cartoon.

Print
answer
here

TO "   "

JUMBLE®

Unscramble these four Jumbles, one letter to each square, to form four ordinary words.

KULCC

HOPNY

CLYMAL

WHERDS

Is that your best price?

$29,000

OFTEN SAID WHEN THE COST IS QUESTIONED.

Now arrange the circled letters to form the surprise answer, as suggested by the above cartoon.

Print answer here

JUMBLE®

Unscramble these four Jumbles, one letter to
each square, to form four ordinary words.

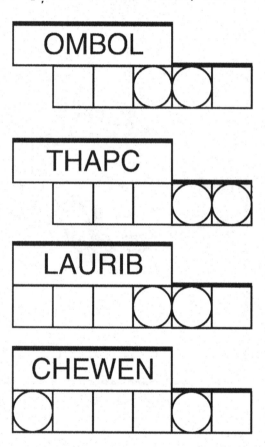

OMBOL

THAPC

LAURIB

CHEWEN

We're going to miss you.

Wow, look at all the pasta dishes.

WHAT THE ITALIAN COUPLE SERVED AT THE GOING AWAY PARTY

Now arrange the circled letters to form the
surprise answer, as suggested by the above
cartoon.

Print answer here

Royal

JUMBLE®

Challenger
Puzzles

JUMBLE®

Unscramble these six Jumbles, one letter to each square, to form six ordinary words.

VEENAL

PHANEP

LAAXYG

GHURNY

GOSTEO

RIEVIL

WHAT THE
BIGAMIST WAS.

Now arrange the circled letters to form the surprise answer, as suggested by the above cartoon.

Print answer here

JUMBLE®

Unscramble these six Jumbles, one letter to each square, to form six ordinary words.

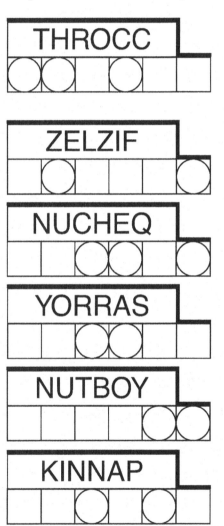

THROCC

ZELZIF

NUCHEQ

YORRAS

NUTBOY

KINNAP

Sit down and be quiet

You're unfair. I demand justice

A ROWDY DEFENDANT CAN DO THIS TO A JUDGE.

Now arrange the circled letters to form the surprise answer, as suggested by the above cartoon.

Print answer here

" ◯◯◯ " ◯◯◯ ◯◯◯◯◯◯◯◯◯

JUMBLE®

Unscramble these six Jumbles, one letter to each square, to form six ordinary words.

LEXNAF

TISMEY

UPKAME

SURDIA

REFILP

SWUINE

Not a word until we do our research

WHAT THE ARCHAEOLOGISTS DID WHEN THEY DISCOVERED THE MUMMY

Now arrange the circled letters to form the surprise answer, as suggested by the above cartoon.

Print answer here

◯◯◯◯◯ IT ◯◯◯◯◯ " ◯◯◯◯◯ "

PUZZLE 163

JUMBLE®

Unscramble these six Jumbles, one letter to each square, to form six ordinary words.

DENORM

NEBING

CULIES

DALLIP

GYLGOO

GENPOS

Seems like a nice fella

Thank you for the kind treatment

WANTED
L.HOYT

LEFT RIGHT

WHEN THE SUSPECT WAS ARRESTED, HE MADE A ---

Now arrange the circled letters to form the surprise answer, as suggested by the above cartoon.

Print answer here

[____] " [_____] "

JUMBLE®

Unscramble these six Jumbles, one letter to
each square, to form six ordinary words.

REEMIP

TUFLAR

TANIAT

GIFNIX

CLARRO

FLUEYE

Oh, this
is the life

WHAT HE ENJOYED
WHEN HE SOLD THE
APPLE ORCHARD

Now arrange the circled letters to form the
surprise answer, as suggested by the above
cartoon.

Print answer here

A " ◯◯◯◯◯◯◯◯◯ " ◯◯◯◯◯◯

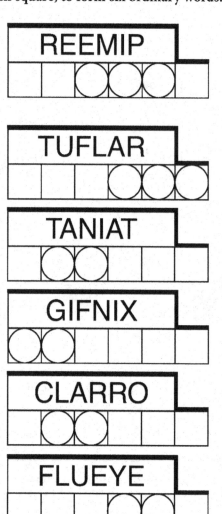

JUMBLE®

Unscramble these six Jumbles, one letter to each square, to form six ordinary words.

INDIGH

TORICE

YAWNAY

RYNTIG

RENCOR

REEBOF

I didn't get the promotion

THE TRAVEL AGENT QUIT HIS JOB BECAUSE HE WASN'T ---

Now arrange the circled letters to form the surprise answer, as suggested by the above cartoon.

Print answer here

JUMBLE®

Unscramble these six Jumbles, one letter to each square, to form six ordinary words.

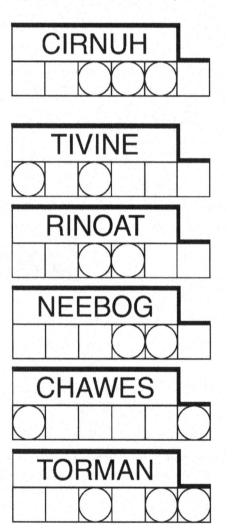

CIRNUH

TIVINE

RINOAT

NEEBOG

CHAWES

TORMAN

I firmly believe that you are guilty

HOW THE JUDGE ADDRESSED THE DEFENDANT.

Now arrange the circled letters to form the surprise answer, as suggested by the above cartoon.

Print answer here

" "

JUMBLE®

Unscramble these six Jumbles, one letter to each square, to form six ordinary words.

DELNAH

SELAMY

HUSTYP

RAGUTI

FOTEEF

ZEFIRE

I think I'll tie one on. **Ha Ha Ha**

HE THOUGHT HE WAS A WIT, BUT THE CLERK THOUGHT HE WAS ---

Now arrange the circled letters to form the surprise answer, as suggested by the above cartoon.

Print answer here

171

JUMBLE®

Unscramble these six Jumbles, one letter to each square, to form six ordinary words.

GUYSAR

TURSIM

LAHMYN

ACCUST

UNJORI

DROLIF

WHAT THE FILM-MAKER AND THE ASTRONOMER HAD IN COMMON.

Now arrange the circled letters to form the surprise answer, as suggested by the above cartoon.

Print answer here

JUMBLE®

Unscramble these six Jumbles, one letter to each square, to form six ordinary words.

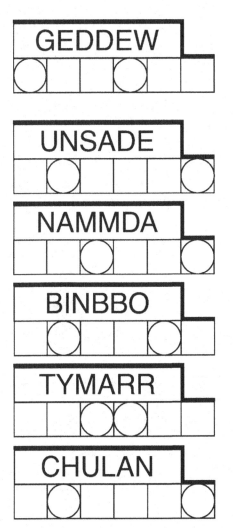

GEDDEW

UNSADE

NAMMDA

BINBBO

TYMARR

CHULAN

He holds the world record

I'm thirsty. Get me some water, NOW!

WHAT THE OLYMPIC STAR LIKED TO THROW.

Now arrange the circled letters to form the surprise answer, as suggested by the above cartoon.

Print answer here

HIS " ◯◯◯◯◯◯ " ◯◯◯◯◯◯◯

JUMBLE®

Unscramble these six Jumbles, one letter to each square, to form six ordinary words.

CLITIA

SPOGLE

JOUFLY

TEPLES

TASTEE

DUCINE

You did the crime, now you do the time. Five years

WHEN THE BURGLAR WAS FOUND GUILTY, THE JUDGE GAVE HIM ---

Now arrange the circled letters to form the surprise answer, as suggested by the above cartoon.

Print answer here

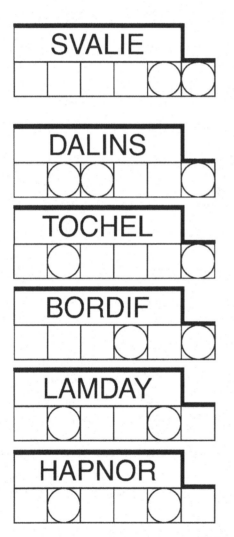

JUMBLE

Unscramble these six Jumbles, one letter to each square, to form six ordinary words.

SVALIE

DALINS

TOCHEL

BORDIF

LAMDAY

HAPNOR

Oh, you motionless sphere. I will send you down the fairway

WHAT THE ORATOR
DID ON THE
GOLF COURSE.

Now arrange the circled letters to form the surprise answer, as suggested by the above cartoon.

Print answer here

" ⬡⬡⬡⬡⬡⬡⬡⬡⬡ " THE ⬡⬡⬡⬡

175

JUMBLE®

Unscramble these six Jumbles, one letter to
each square, to form six ordinary words.

ERTOPY

CORCUN

GOBNEY

RANCOY

BUNNIO

YOWHLL

Can you spare
some change?

ANOTHER NAME
FOR A PANHANDLER.

Now arrange the circled letters to form the
surprise answer, as suggested by the above
cartoon.

Print answer here

A

JUMBLE®

Unscramble these six Jumbles, one letter to
each square, to form six ordinary words.

CIPCIN

DYKLIN

REKALT

DACLUN

MABOOB

DEGELP

Sir, I believe my work merits a salary increase

Yes, it does

WHEN HE ASKED HIS BOSS FOR A RAISE, HE WAS ---

Now arrange the circled letters to form the
surprise answer, as suggested by the above
cartoon.

Print answer here

 AND " "

JUMBLE®

Unscramble these six Jumbles, one letter to each square, to form six ordinary words.

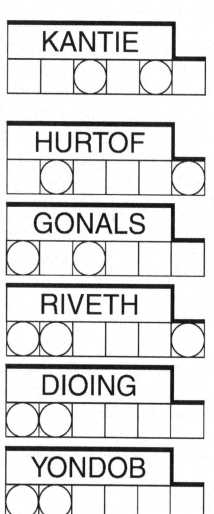

KANTIE

HURTOF

GONALS

RIVETH

DIOING

YONDOB

Watch it, champ!

OW!

TONIGHT

WHAT THE BOXER DID WHEN HE TRIPPED IN THE LOCKER ROOM.

Now arrange the circled letters to form the surprise answer, as suggested by the above cartoon.

Print answer here

IT

JUMBLE®

Unscramble these six Jumbles, one letter to each square, to form six ordinary words.

FRIPOT

VYCOON

HAWRTT

BITTID

TEICED

SHURTH

I've had it. Let's get a pizza

THE STUDENT PUT AWAY THE DICTIONARY BECAUSE HE WAS ----

Now arrange the circled letters to form the surprise answer, as suggested by the above cartoon.

Print answer here

FOR "◯◯◯◯◯"

JUMBLE®

Unscramble these six Jumbles, one letter to
each square, to form six ordinary words.

NOOPUC

PARULL

ZARWID

POMCLE

DORIAH

UNTARE

Dawn to dusk,
seven days
a week

WHAT THE FARMER
HAD TO DO TO
MAKE ENDS MEET.

Now arrange the circled letters to form the
surprise answer, as suggested by the above
cartoon.

Print answer here

JUMBLE®

Unscramble these six Jumbles, one letter to each square, to form six ordinary words.

LANSID

INBOUN

LEEXAH

CAFFEE

YOBLUD

NARFIA

Watch out, slow down!

HOW HE DROVE
WITH HIS
MOTHER-IN-LAW IN
THE BACK SEAT.

Now arrange the circled letters to form the surprise answer, as suggested by the above cartoon.

Print answer here

THE " "

JUMBLE®

Unscramble these six Jumbles, one letter to each square, to form six ordinary words.

THIBLE

BLOTEG

PHYSEC

RYNWIT

MADORR

MNOMOC

Your claim is dismissed

Sorry, here's my bill

Why, you incompetent..

WHAT A LAWYER CAN GET WHEN HE LOSES A CASE.

Now arrange the circled letters to form the surprise answer, as suggested by the above cartoon.

Print answer here

⬡⬡⬡⬡⬡ ' ⬡ ⬡⬡⬡⬡⬡⬡⬡ TO ⬡⬡⬡

JUMBLE®

Unscramble these six Jumbles, one letter to each square, to form six ordinary words.

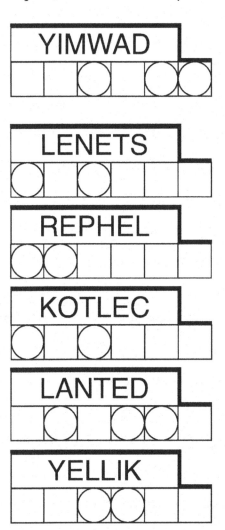

YIMWAD

LENETS

REPHEL

KOTLEC

LANTED

YELLIK

Usually you flop on stage.

Hey, this is fun!

WHEN THE COMEDIAN JUMPED FROM THE LOFT, HE EXPERIENCED A ---

Now arrange the circled letters to form the surprise answer, as suggested by the above cartoon.

Print answer here

" ⬡⬡⬡⬡⬡⬡ " IN A ⬡⬡⬡⬡⬡⬡⬡⬡

Answers

1. **Jumbles:** BLOAT SHEAF TUMULT FRUGAL
   Answer: When the speed team prepared for the big drag race, they went — FULL "THROTTLE"

2. **Jumbles:** ENSUE FLANK FILLET PRAYER
   Answer: What he saw when he visited the print shop — ALL "TYPES"

3. **Jumbles:** BLAZE ELDER GRUBBY INVENT
   Answer: What the delivery man turned into on his wedding day — A "BELLE" RINGER

4. **Jumbles:** THINK GUEST MINGLE CAUGHT
   Answer: Enjoyed by the couple when the power failed — "LIGHT" MUSIC

5. **Jumbles:** POWER DUNCE BUSHEL SURETY
   Answer: What the running back did as time was running out — "RUSHED" TO SCORE

6. **Jumbles:** LIGHT AROMA DETAIN GASKET
   Answer: What the pupils experienced when they failed the multiplication test — HARD "TIMES"

7. **Jumbles:** QUEST NUDGE SADIST JURIST
   Answer: When the twins ate Mom's party cupcakes, they got their — JUST "DESSERTS"

8. **Jumbles:** OUTDO PLUME SCHOOL FASTEN
   Answer: You might say the "hot" movie did this to the matrons — LEFT THEM "COLD"

9. **Jumbles:** QUEER COLIC HOPPER PUSHER
   Answer: Where the fisherman could always be found — ON HIS PERCH PERCH

10. **Jumbles:** EVENT SAVOR BUCKLE BUTLER
    Answer: A good carpenter will do this — HIS "LEVEL" BEST

11. **Jumbles:** LADLE SHEEP ABUSED CLOVEN
    Answer: What the barber experienced on his way to work — A CLOSE "SHAVE"

12. **Jumbles:** ORBIT TESTY SAILOR TANKER
    Answer: What the recruit did when bayonet training began — TOOK A "STAB" AT IT

13. **Jumbles:** RAVEN QUASH BUBBLE UNRULY
    Answer: What a Londoner uses for a "line" — A "QUEUE"

14. **Jumbles:** DELVE CYNIC AERATE QUAVER
    Answer: When the novice was taught how to focus, the instructions were — QUITE "CLEAR"

15. **Jumbles:** INLET PENCE INVADE OSSIFY
    Answer: What the boy experienced when he was fitted for a suit — PINS AND NEEDLES

16. **Jumbles:** KEYED GUMMY ELICIT FINISH
    Answer: What she decided when the eye doctor asked her out — TO "SEE" HIM

17. **Jumbles:** SMOKY LOFTY GLOOMY LOTION
    Answer: When he was told about the hole in the wall, the cop said he'd — "LOOK" INTO IT

18. **Jumbles:** PANSY CAPON FUTURE BOUGHT
    Answer: What the photographer used to take pictures of the new car — "AUTO" FOCUS

19. **Jumbles:** LURID FORAY MORTAR BEWARE
    Answer: Can be alone when locked up — A YEAR OR TWO

20. **Jumbles:** BATHE ELUDE ZENITH BARIUM
    Answer: Why the fighter pilot refused to tour the submarine — IT WAS "BENEATH" HIM

21. **Jumbles:** DRONE MONEY EMBARK OBJECT
    Answer: Can be knitted while mending — A BROKEN BONE

22. **Jumbles:** BROIL MOSSY WISELY MAGNET
    Answer: How he performed in the lifeguard test — "SWIMMINGLY"

23. **Jumbles:** CHASM LAPEL ASTHMA STUDIO
    Answer: When the tipsy partygoer wore a lampshade, his wife said he'd — LOST HIS HEAD

24. **Jumbles:** GOUGE FRANC FLAUNT KINGLY
    Answer: When the stripper learned to fly, she was good at this — TAKING OFF

25. **Jumbles:** INKED GLOVE HEARSE HOTBED
    Answer: What the knitter did when she made the sleeves uneven — "NEEDLED" HER

26. **Jumbles:** SCOUR GULLY UNSOLD NEARLY
    Answer: The producer entered the marathon race because he was good at — LONG "RUNS"

27. **Jumbles:** MOTIF TANGY IMBUED SATIRE
    Answer: When she refused to pay for her portrait, he turned into a — "MAD" ARTIST

28. **Jumbles:** FAUNA CURVE EMBRYO INTENT
    Answer: When the shopper was accused of passing phony money, he had a — COUNTER FIT

29. **Jumbles:** OFTEN LOUSE LIZARD MARROW
    Answer: When the goose feathers flew up and away, they were — STILL "DOWN"

30. **Jumbles:** GAVEL TULIP CIRCUS MAGPIE
    Answer: "Pirates" can give you this — SEA TRIP

31. **Jumbles:** SKULK CROUP MODISH NOUGAT
    Answer: What the cat show winner turned into — A GLAMOUR "PUSS"

32. **Jumbles:** BATON FORGO HUMBLE COWARD
    Answer: When the icicle fell on the mailman's head, he was — OUT "COLD"

33. **Jumbles:** FAVOR CEASE JARGON DRIVEL
    Answer: The waiter won the tennis match because he was a — GOOD "SERVER"

34. **Jumbles:** LYRIC PIETY FLORAL PEPSIN
    Answer: The actor used greasepaint because he had a — "SLIPPERY" ROLE

35. **Jumbles:** FISHY BEIGE ENZYME FACILE
    Answer: Advice that isn't sound — SILENCE

36. **Jumbles:** CAPON BURST NETHER PRIMER
    Answer: It takes more than one to run this kind of business — A PARTNERSHIP

37. **Jumbles:** LOUSE RAINY OPPOSE FORGET
    Answer: On a golf course, many rich guys can be — "POOR" PLAYERS

38. **Jumbles:** FIFTY IRATE HOMAGE KIMONO
    Answer: What his wife did when she picked out a watch — TOOK HER "TIME"

39. **Jumbles:** DOWNY MINER TAWDRY JOBBER
    Answer: What the student who wanted to be an author did — WROTE FOR MONEY

40. **Jumbles:** TRUTH GRAVE HEARTH THROAT
    Answer: How he described the talk with his cardiologist — HEART TO HEART

41. **Jumbles:** SINGE PECAN FIXING SURETY
    Answer: When she requested a song, the guitarist had it at his — FINGERTIPS

42. **Jumbles:** FAITH SAUTE STURDY DEVOUR
    Answer: What the mobster faced when he planted the trees — A "SHADY" FUTURE

43. **Jumbles:** SHYLY WALTZ LATEST FERVID
    Answer: For most people, obituaries are this — LAST "WRITES"

44. **Jumbles:** SNORT CEASE SOIREE BEFALL
    Answer: You can find this marked down in a department store — AN ESCALATOR

45. **Jumbles:** CABIN PATIO KILLER POSTAL
    Answer: What the students brought to school for their mean teacher — "CRAB" APPLES

46. **Jumbles:** PILOT AFTER MILDEW WHITEN
    Answer: The golddigger snubbed the handsome partygoer because he wasn't — WORTH HER "WILE"

47. **Jumbles:** RIVET TRYST VOYAGE EYEFUL
Answer: What a ringing alarm clock can do —
GIVE YOU A "START"

48. **Jumbles:** AFIRE BALKY BUTLER SAILOR
Answer: After paying for the tire change, he was —
"FLAT" BROKE

49. **Jumbles:** CHUTE HEAVY BANDIT LIQUOR
Answer: What the tree trimmers did when they got the big
job — "BRANCHED" OUT

50. **Jumbles:** BASSO TUNED MODEST TYCOON
Answer: When the tipsy caveman got home, he was —
STONED AND STONED

51. **Jumbles:** PIANO KNELL MAGNUM FARINA
Answer: Important to have when you go hunting —
A "GAME" PLAN

52. **Jumbles:** TARRY PEACE TANDEM PREFIX
Answer: What the film student received when he appeared
in the movie — "EXTRA" CREDIT

53. **Jumbles:** SWOOP BULGY DEBTOR TRIBAL
Answer: What the farm family ended up with during the
drought — A DUST BOWL

54. **Jumbles:** APART DELVE FALLOW BAKERY
Answer: When the banker's glass of beer spilled over, the
bartender said it was an — OVER "DRAFT"

55. **Jumbles:** SYLPH IDIOT FINISH TRAGIC
Answer: What the gabby barber did — GOT IN HIS "HAIR"

56. **Jumbles:** COMET PAPER BLITHE BUSILY
Answer: What the dentist did for the charity event —
PUT THE "BITE" ON HIM

57. **Jumbles:** NAVAL QUEEN SYMBOL RITUAL
Answer: What the military couple needed to see the fall
colors — AUTUMN "LEAVES"

58. **Jumbles:** KITTY BANDY GARLIC PALLID
Answer: She quit working at the coffee shop because of the
— DAILY "GRIND"

59. **Jumbles:** MANLY PARKA TROPHY FASTEN
Answer: What the space walker resorted to when a tool
floated away — "EARTHY" TALK

60. **Jumbles:** GAUZE NERVY SEETHE BUCKET
Answer: She drew the brainy student's attention with this —
HER EYE CUE

61. **Jumbles:** ACUTE INLET OPAQUE PURVEY
Answer: When the witches played poker, they had —
QUITE A "POT"

62. **Jumbles:** HOIST DOUGH SPLEEN GENTRY
Answer: How the trumpet player managed to join the
exclusive gathering — HE "HORNED" IN

63. **Jumbles:** ARDOR SUITE CHOSEN SCORCH
Answer: When Dad gave his teenager a driving lesson, it
turned into — A "CRASH" COURSE

64. **Jumbles:** FAULT DOGMA EFFIGY TYPING
Answer: How a ski trip can end up — END UP

65. **Jumbles:** FUZZY CAKED PURITY ASYLUM
Answer: Important for a pinup girl to be this — STUCK UP

66. **Jumbles:** BROOD AGING MORBID BRANCH
Answer: Another name for an ornithologist —
A "BIRD BRAIN"

67. **Jumbles:** WOMEN ERUPT ENSIGN INCOME
Answer: He traded in his watch because it was —
"TIME" FOR A NEW ONE

68. **Jumbles:** MOURN WRATH COUPLE RENDER
Answer: When the campers got caught in a heavy
cloudburst, it felt like — A "DROWN" POUR

69. **Jumbles:** PIECE YOUNG COUSIN DULCET
Answer: What the stockbrokers gave the attentive waiter —
A GOOD "TIP"

70. **Jumbles:** BUXOM TOPAZ BALLET COMPLY
Answer: The new parents learned how to take care of the
baby from the — BOTTOM UP

71. **Jumbles:** PENCE DUCAT PUNDIT UNHOOK
Answer: What the quack doctor did when the police
arrived — "DUCKED" OUT

72. **Jumbles:** TAWNY BEIGE HARDLY COOPER
Answer: What Mom did when she dried her hair —
BLEW HER "TOP"

73. **Jumbles:** FAINT YOKEL MIDWAY JUMPER
Answer: When a computer fails, it can be — "TERMINAL"

74. **Jumbles:** BRAWL FEIGN NUDISM DAMPEN
Answer: When the couple couldn't afford a vacation, they let
their — MINDS "WANDER"

75. **Jumbles:** HYENA TAFFY EYELET FACING
Answer: What the couple enjoyed when they were bumped
to first class — A FLIGHT OF "FANCY"

76. **Jumbles:** FOIST LUCID EMERGE REDUCE
Answer: How the team felt when their coach growled at
them all day — DOG-TIRED

77. **Jumbles:** LIMIT DITTO BAFFLE WISELY
Answer: What her aging husband faced when he decided to
diet — A "WAIST" OF TIME

78. **Jumbles:** SMOKY LIVEN DECADE FRENZY
Answer: The farmer said the downpour was —
A "SODDEN" RAIN

79. **Jumbles:** BROOK MONEY FAMILY SHREWD
Answer: What the senator did when he got the floor —
RAISED THE ROOF

80. **Jumbles:** DUSKY RIGOR MORTAR JACKAL
Answer: When the geologist made an important discovery,
he became a — "ROCK" STAR

81. **Jumbles:** GOING LIGHT DURESS PAROLE
Answer: One way to solve a knotty problem —
PULL STRINGS

82. **Jumbles:** USURP APPLY POWDER BEHELD
Answer: What the clerk got when she decorated the gift
package — "WRAPPED" UP IN IT

83. **Jumbles:** LOFTY BIPED DROWSY BARREN
Answer: When service was slow, the hungry diners became
— "WAITERS"

84. **Jumbles:** MADLY NOBLE ZODIAC PAYING
Answer: When he caught Junior playing with matches, Dad
was — BLAZING MAD

85. **Jumbles:** ELUDE WIPED UPTOWN OUTING
Answer: What Mom did when her son cut his hand —
WOUND THE WOUND

86. **Jumbles:** DOUSE DAISY BISHOP ACCENT
Answer: When the railbird bet on the long shot, it was an —
"ODDS" CHOICE

87. **Jumbles:** CRAZE USURY JUGGLE BOILED
Answer: How the professor got his doctorate — BY DEGREES

88. **Jumbles:** ROACH UNIFY POMADE DIGEST
Answer: What the stranded boaters came up with to get off
the island — A "RAFT" OF IDEAS

89. **Jumbles:** CHASM BANJO POLLEN BEAUTY
Answer: The zookeeper described cleaning the lion cage
as — A "BEASTLY" JOB

90. **Jumbles:** SOUSE ANISE TYPHUS UPROAR
Answer: What the counterfeiter said when he was
confronted by the reporter — STOP THE PRESSES

91. **Jumbles:** GAUDY WHOOP RATIFY JUNGLE
Answer: The couple left the restaurant because the
accordion music was — "DRAWN" OUT

92. **Jumbles:** HOVEL VISOR BLOUSE DECENT
Answer: What the couple said when the poetry reading left
them puzzled — COULD BE "VERSE"

93. **Jumbles:** ELDER PURGE EXOTIC PENCIL
Answer: When they asked for a room, the hotel clerk was —
PREOCCUPIED

185

94. **Jumbles:** JOUST FANCY PAYOFF UNSOLD
Answer: What the runner ate before the big race —
"FAST" FOOD

95. **Jumbles:** PAYEE DICED SLEEPY AVOWAL
Answer: The mortician's wife visited the beauty parlor
because it was a — PLACE TO "DYE"

96. **Jumbles:** MOUSY AZURE GUIDED IMMUNE
Answer: When the pupil told the class what he did on
vacation, he — "SUMMER-IZED" IT

97. **Jumbles:** GNOME CRUSH POCKET WEASEL
Answer: What they got when they worked in the coffee
shop — LOTS OF "PERKS"

98. **Jumbles:** TEMPO ALIAS HANSOM LAWYER
Answer: When he didn't fix the leak, his wife said it was a —
SHOWER "STALL"

99. **Jumbles:** WHISK GLEAM SONATA CAMPUS
Answer: Easy to do with your neighbors when you build a
swimming pool — MAKE A "SPLASH"

100. **Jumbles:** FLOOR BATCH FLUNKY LEAVEN
Answer: What the chimney sweep had to deal with —
THE "FLUE"

101. **Jumbles:** JETTY STOOP INTENT PERSON
Answer: What his wife did and was when she shopped all
day — SPENT AND SPENT

102. **Jumbles:** AMITY MINER HARROW AWEIGH
Answer: The archery competition was won by an —
ARROW MARGIN

103. **Jumbles:** GUEST NOTCH PELVIS LACKEY
Answer: The college football player gave up the pigskin
when it was time for this — THE SHEEPSKIN

104. **Jumbles:** KNACK TYPED MUFFLE POLICY
Answer: Why the bookkeeper received a raise —
HE "COUNTED"

105. **Jumbles:** SKUNK TWEAK GAMBOL ADJOIN
Answer: The plastic surgeon sought the clerk's help because
she had a — "KNOWS" JOB

106. **Jumbles:** CLOAK STUNG OUTCRY BODICE
Answer: The electrician joined the baseball team because
he — COULD "SOCKET"

107. **Jumbles:** ADAPT SAUTE CALLOW BEGONE
Answer: What the defense lawyer wanted the plaintiff to
do — SETTLE "DOWN"

108. **Jumbles:** WINCE TRULY LIZARD WAYLAY
Answer: They were motivated to hunt for snakes by the —
"CRAWL" OF THE WILD

109. **Jumbles:** BURLY FEINT UPHELD BIGAMY
Answer: When the foreman said he was all wrong, the
workers said he was — ALL RIGHT

110. **Jumbles:** BOWER MAIZE MEMORY TRAGIC
Answer: The graffiti vandal was arrested for a —
GRIME CRIME

111. **Jumbles:** DAUNT SWOOP BEAGLE ESTATE
Answer: What the night owl did day after day —
WENT TO SLEEP

112. **Jumbles:** WHOSE BORAX HUMBLE SLEIGH
Answer: Shot by the television host on the safari —
A "GAME" SHOW

113. **Jumbles:** SPURN FLUTE WEAPON NOVICE
Answer: Easy to turn a fifty into — A PEN AND TWO FIVES

114. **Jumbles:** PLAIT UTTER SCRIBE CANDID
Answer: When their team lost the big game, the home crowd
was — IN "TIERS"

115. **Jumbles:** COUPE TAKEN PACKET NORMAL
Answer: What the bartender did when the disagreement got
heated — KEPT HIS COOL

116. **Jumbles:** GLORY CAKED GRIMLY WEEVIL
Answer: Why the pickle maker decided to quit —
IT WAS "DILL" WORK

117. **Jumbles:** GUILD ACRID MARLIN AVENUE
Answer: The couple went for a spin in the storm because it
was — "DRIVING" RAIN

118. **Jumbles:** DECRY ROBOT SUNDAE VERIFY
Answer: When the exhausted spy went to bed, he was —
UNDER COVER

119. **Jumbles:** IMBUE LEAFY GARISH OXYGEN
Answer: What Mom got from "one hug" — ENOUGH

120. **Jumbles:** UNCLE TEPID GYPSUM RUBBER
Answer: Another name for a great magician —
A SUPER "DUPER"

121. **Jumbles:** GAMUT PATIO GASKET MARTYR
Answer: What the warden gave the repeat offender —
A TIME "OUT"

122. **Jumbles:** LOONY BLAZE LATEST ZIGZAG
Answer: The driver won the road race because he knew —
ALL THE ANGLES

123. **Jumbles:** AGONY RABBI PARADE DISMAY
Answer: What she ran into at the water cooler —
A BIG "DRIP"

124. **Jumbles:** SURLY FRAUD NUMBER BUSHEL
Answer: What the city fathers used to clean up after the
winter storm — A "SLUSH" FUND

125. **Jumbles:** GLADE DUSKY BABIED HYMNAL
Answer: When her client was arrested for forgery, the
clairvoyant said it was — A BAD "SIGN"

126. **Jumbles:** VALVE SNORT BUCKLE ORPHAN
Answer: What the storekeeper wanted for a keg of
beer — CASH ON THE BARREL

127. **Jumbles:** SYLPH NIECE GOSPEL CHOSEN
Answer: What happened to the politician when the
teleprompter failed — HE WAS "SPEECHLESS"

128. **Jumbles:** SYNOD EXERT PEPSIN DISOWN
Answer: What he did when he heard his wife shriek —
STEPPED ON IT

129. **Jumbles:** GAVEL FUNNY POPLIN HEIFER
Answer: When the comedian gained weight, he tried to —
LAUGH IT OFF

130. **Jumbles:** LUSTY PECAN BALLAD STICKY
Answer: What the witch did on the fishing trip —
"CAST" A SPELL

131. **Jumbles:** BLANK LEECH CANNED BYWORD
Answer: When the spy made a secret call, he — HAD A CODE

132. **Jumbles:** WHINE BONES EXCITE KINGLY
Answer: When she bought another pillbox hat, her husband
said it was — "SICKENING"

133. **Jumbles:** RAPID POACH ALKALI BARROW
Answer: For some, an unpopular way of making money —
HARD WORK

134. **Jumbles:** FILMY CHUTE DISCUS VALISE
Answer: What Mom made him do when he was late for his
piano lesson — FACE THE MUSIC

135. **Jumbles:** FLORA FORAY EMPLOY IMPORT
Answer: The pancake cook was fired because he was a —
FLIP FLOP

136. **Jumbles:** LATCH HIKER ENCORE BREACH
Answer: Who they got married to — EACH OTHER

137. **Jumbles:** DOWDY GRIMY IMPEND BROKEN
Answer: What the down-and-out handyman did when he
needed cash — "WIRED" FOR MONEY

138. **Jumbles:** SOOTY FOIST PURIFY NOZZLE
Answer: A good strategy for a pocket billiards team —
"POOL" THEIR EFFORTS

139. **Jumbles:** PILOT AFTER KINDLY FILLET
Answer: What he turned his car into — A "TINKER" TOY

140. **Jumbles:** MADAM EIGHT JITNEY MIDDAY
Answer: How she felt when the plane bounced around in the
storm — "AGITATED"

141. **Jumbles:** TWINE FLUKE SURTAX FASTEN
    Answer: The hunter hired the taxidermist because he — KNEW HIS "STUFF"

142. **Jumbles:** ENVOY HOIST BAZAAR MISFIT
    Answer: What she experienced on her date with the eye doctor — "I" STRAIN

143. **Jumbles:** MERGE BANDY LIQUID TARTAR
    Answer: How he felt when he unplugged the sink — "DRAINED"

144. **Jumbles:** SWOON GRIPE PULPIT SPLEEN
    Answer: A politician will do this when faced with a knotty problem — PULL "STRINGS"

145. **Jumbles:** UNWED RIVET HELIUM PURITY
    Answer: What her friend did to shorten the long story — INTERRUPTED

146. **Jumbles:** CYNIC LIMBO TEAPOT PARDON
    Answer: The arctic explorer said his head gear was a — POLAR ICE CAP

147. **Jumbles:** ARDOR PIANO SCROLL JAGGED
    Answer: What it can take to put up with bad manners — GOOD ONES

148. **Jumbles:** LEGAL DANDY SQUALL NAPKIN
    Answer: Although the bachelor owned a large farm, the girls said he was — "UNLANDED"

149. **Jumbles:** WEIGH TITLE MOHAIR POWDER
    Answer: When the class did the puzzle, the teacher had a — WORD WITH THEM

150. **Jumbles:** AFIRE COWER VASSAL BISECT
    Answer: What the doctor used when his desk chair squeaked — CASTER OIL

151. **Jumbles:** HONOR EMPTY BELLOW PRISON
    Answer: The forecaster was weather wise, but the golfers considered him — OTHERWISE

152. **Jumbles:** AXIOM DOGMA UNSAID HELMET
    Answer: What they ended up with at the greyhound races — "HOT" DOGS

153. **Jumbles:** MESSY BEFIT BODILY TUSSLE
    Answer: A joke will get the most laughs when the — BOSS TELLS IT

154. **Jumbles:** PRIZE DROOP MEMBER MUSCLE
    Answer: What the farmer acquired when he bought the junkyard — A "BUMPER" CROP

155. **Jumbles:** QUASH LURID BRANCH AROUND
    Answer: The manicurist said nails are this — "HARD" ON THE HANDS

156. **Jumbles:** RURAL WOMEN ESTATE TERROR
    Answer: What the groomer lost on his wedding day — TWO LETTERS

157. **Jumbles:** TAWNY FOLIO UPSHOT SUBWAY
    Answer: When spring planting was completed, the farmer said it was — SOW, SOW

158. **Jumbles:** DUCAT WAFER SCHEME PIRATE
    Answer: What the picnickers did during the tug of war — TRIED TO "WREST"

159. **Jumbles:** CLUCK PHONY CALMLY SHREWD
    Answer: Often said when the cost is questioned — HOW MUCH?

160. **Jumbles:** BLOOM PATCH BURIAL WHENCE
    Answer: What the Italian couple served at the going away party — CIAO CHOW

161. **Jumbles:** LEAVEN HAPPEN GALAXY HUNGRY STOOGE VIRILE
    Answer: What the bigamist was — VERY "ENGAGING"

162. **Jumbles:** CROTCH FIZZLE QUENCH ROSARY BOUNTY NAPKIN
    Answer: A rowdy defendant can do this to a judge — "TRY" HIS PATIENCE

163. **Jumbles:** FLAXEN STYMIE MAKEUP RADIUS PILFER UNWISE
    Answer: What the archaeologists did when they discovered the mummy — KEPT IT UNDER WRAPS

164. **Jumbles:** MODERN BENIGN SLUICE PALLID GOOGLY SPONGE
    Answer: When the suspect was arrested, he made a — GOOD "IMPRESSION"

165. **Jumbles:** EMPIRE ARTFUL ATTAIN FIXING CORRAL EYEFUL
    Answer: What he enjoyed when he sold the apple orchard — A "FRUITFUL" PROFIT

166. **Jumbles:** HIDING EROTIC ANYWAY TRYING CORNER BEFORE
    Answer: The travel agent quit his job because he wasn't — "GOING" ANYWHERE

167. **Jumbles:** URCHIN INVITE RATION BEGONE CASHEW MATRON
    Answer: How the judge addressed the defendant — WITH "CONVICTION"

168. **Jumbles:** HANDLE MEASLY TYPHUS GUITAR TOFFEE FRIEZE
    Answer: He thought he was a wit, but the clerk thought he was — ONLY HALF RIGHT

169. **Jumbles:** SUGARY TRUISM HYMNAL CACTUS JUNIOR FLORID
    Answer: What the filmmaker and the astronomer had in common — SHOOTING STARS

170. **Jumbles:** WEDGED SUNDAE MADMAN BOBBIN MARTYR LAUNCH
    Answer: What the Olympic star liked to throw — HIS "WEIGHT" AROUND

171. **Jumbles:** ITALIC GOSPEL JOYFUL PESTLE ESTATE INDUCE
    Answer: When the burglar was found guilty, the judge gave him — POETIC JUSTICE

172. **Jumbles:** VALISE ISLAND CLOTHE FORBID MALADY ORPHAN
    Answer: What the orator did on the golf course — "ADDRESSED" THE BALL

173. **Jumbles:** POETRY CONCUR BYGONE CRAYON BUNION WHOLLY
    Answer: Another name for a panhandler — A COIN COLLECTOR

174. **Jumbles:** PICNIC KINDLY TALKER UNCLAD BAMBOO PLEDGE
    Answer: When he asked his boss for a raise, he was — CALM AND "COLLECTED"

175. **Jumbles:** INTAKE FOURTH SLOGAN THRIVE INDIGO NOBODY
    Answer: What the boxer did when he tripped in the locker room — TOOK IT ON THE SHIN

176. **Jumbles:** PROFIT CONVOY THWART TIDBIT DECEIT THRUSH
    Answer: The student put away the dictionary because he was — TOO TIRED FOR WORDS

177. **Jumbles:** COUPON PLURAL WIZARD COMPEL HAIRDO NATURE
    Answer: What the farmer had to do to make ends meet — PRODUCE PRODUCE

178. **Jumbles:** ISLAND BUNION EXHALE EFFACE DOUBLY FARINA
    Answer: How he drove with his mother-in-law in the back seat — UNDER THE "INFLUENCE"

179. **Jumbles:** BLITHE GOBLET PSYCHE WINTRY RAMROD COMMON
    Answer: What a lawyer can get when he loses a case — WHAT'S COMING TO HIM

180. **Jumbles:** MIDWAY NESTLE HELPER LOCKET DENTAL LIKELY
    Answer: When the comedian jumped from the loft, he experienced a — "NEEDLE" IN A HAYSTACK

Need More Jumbles®?

Jumble® Books

More than 175 puzzles each!

Cowboy Jumble®
$10.95 • ISBN: 978-1-62937-355-3

Jammin' Jumble®
$9.95 • ISBN: 978-1-57243-844-6

Java Jumble®
$10.95 • ISBN: 978-1-60078-415-6

Jet Set Jumble®
$9.95 • ISBN: 978-1-60078-353-1

Jolly Jumble®
$10.95 • ISBN: 978-1-60078-214-5

Jumble® Anniversary
$10.95 • ISBN: 987-1-62937-734-6

Jumble® Ballet
$10.95 • ISBN: 978-1-62937-616-5

Jumble® Birthday
$10.95 • ISBN: 978-1-62937-652-3

Jumble® Celebration
$10.95 • ISBN: 978-1-60078-134-6

Jumble® Champion
$10.95 • ISBN: 978-1-62937-870-1

Jumble® Cuisine
$10.95 • ISBN: 978-1-62937-735-3

Jumble® Drag Race
$9.95 • ISBN: 978-1-62937-483-3

Jumble® Ever After
$10.95 • ISBN: 978-1-62937-785-8

Jumble® Explorer
$9.95 • ISBN: 978-1-60078-854-3

Jumble® Explosion
$10.95 • ISBN: 978-1-60078-078-3

Jumble® Fever
$9.95 • ISBN: 978-1-57243-593-3

Jumble® Galaxy
$10.95 • ISBN: 978-1-60078-583-2

Jumble® Garden
$10.95 • ISBN: 978-1-62937-653-0

Jumble® Genius
$10.95 • ISBN: 978-1-57243-896-5

Jumble® Geography
$10.95 • ISBN: 978-1-62937-615-8

Jumble® Getaway
$10.95 • ISBN: 978-1-60078-547-4

Jumble® Gold
$10.95 • ISBN: 978-1-62937-354-6

Jumble® Jackpot
$10.95 • ISBN: 978-1-57243-897-2

Jumble® Jailbreak
$9.95 • ISBN: 978-1-62937-002-6

Jumble® Jambalaya
$9.95 • ISBN: 978-1-60078-294-7

Jumble® Jitterbug
$10.95 • ISBN: 978-1-60078-584-9

Jumble® Journey
$10.95 • ISBN: 978-1-62937-549-6

Jumble® Jubilation
$10.95 • ISBN: 978-1-62937-784-1

Jumble® Jubilee
$10.95 • ISBN: 978-1-57243-231-4

Jumble® Juggernaut
$9.95 • ISBN: 978-1-60078-026-4

Jumble® Kingdom
$10.95 • ISBN: 978-1-62937-079-8

Jumble® Knockout
$9.95 • ISBN: 978-1-62937-078-1

Jumble® Madness
$10.95 • ISBN: 978-1-892049-24-7

Jumble® Magic
$9.95 • ISBN: 978-1-60078-795-9

Jumble® Mania
$10.95 • ISBN: 978-1-57243-697-8

Jumble® Marathon
$9.95 • ISBN: 978-1-60078-944-1

Jumble® Neighbor
$10.95 • ISBN: 978-1-62937-845-9

Jumble® Parachute
$10.95 • ISBN: 978-1-62937-548-9

Jumble® Safari
$9.95 • ISBN: 978-1-60078-675-4

Jumble® Sensation
$10.95 • ISBN: 978-1-60078-548-1

Jumble® Skyscraper
$10.95 • ISBN: 978-1-62937-869-5

Jumble® Symphony
$10.95 • ISBN: 978-1-62937-131-3

Jumble® Theater
$9.95 • ISBN: 978-1-62937-484-0

Jumble® University
$10.95 • ISBN: 978-1-62937-001-9

Jumble® Unleashed
$10.95 • ISBN: 978-1-62937-844-2

Jumble® Vacation
$10.95 • ISBN: 978-1-60078-796-6

Jumble® Wedding
$9.95 • ISBN: 978-1-62937-307-2

Jumble® Workout
$10.95 • ISBN: 978-1-60078-943-4

Jump, Jive and Jumble®
$9.95 • ISBN: 978-1-60078-215-2

Lunar Jumble®
$9.95 • ISBN: 978-1-60078-853-6

Monster Jumble®
$10.95 • ISBN: 978-1-62937-213-6

Mystic Jumble®
$9.95 • ISBN: 978-1-62937-130-6

Rainy Day Jumble®
$10.95 • ISBN: 978-1-60078-352-4

Royal Jumble®
$10.95 • ISBN: 978-1-60078-738-6

Sports Jumble®
$10.95 • ISBN: 978-1-57243-113-3

Summer Fun Jumble®
$10.95 • ISBN: 978-1-57243-114-0

Touchdown Jumble®
$9.95 • ISBN: 978-1-62937-212-9

Oversize Jumble® Books

More than 500 puzzles!

Colossal Jumble®
$19.95 • ISBN: 978-1-57243-490-5

Jumbo Jumble®
$19.95 • ISBN: 978-1-57243-314-4

Jumble® Crosswords™

More than 175 puzzles!

Jumble® Crosswords™
$10.95 • ISBN: 978-1-57243-347-2